"BIPOLAR IS AN ILLNESS
*NOT* A HOPELESS
DESTINATION
IT CAN BE MAINTAINED
WITH PROPER MEDICATION"
— STANLEY VICTOR PASKAVICH

# Bipolar Disorder A Guide for Parents Told By A Mother.

"SUDDENLY I WANTED TO GET BETTER. MANIA WASN'T FUN ANYMORE. IT WASN'T CREATIVE OR VISIONARY. IT WAS MEAN PARODY AT BEST, A CHEAP CHEMICAL TRICK. I NEEDED TO STOP AND GET BETTER. I'D TAKE WHATEVER THEY GAVE ME, I PLEDGED SILENTLY. I'D TAKE TRILAFON OR THORAZINE OR WHATEVER. I JUST WANTED TO SLEEP."

– DAVID LOVELACE

Provisions and Conditions

**LEGAL NOTICE**

Due to the continuously changing nature of the Internet, the publisher has endeavored to  be as accurate and thorough as possible in creating this document. However, she does not  warrant or represent at any time that the contents are correct.

While every effort has been made to ensure the accuracy of the content in this publication, the publisher is not responsible for any errors, omissions, or interpretations that are  antithetical to the subject matter.

Any apparent slights on particular individuals, groups,  or institutions are inadvertent.

As with anything else in life, the reader is asked to act based on his or her own judgment and the specifics of the situation.

*This book doesn't advocate any medical advice.*
*The author writes only as someone who lives with bipolar on a daily basis in her home.*
*This is her story and a collection of stories told to her or found from authentic sources.*
*Anyone with symptoms of mental illness, who reads this should get help from their*
*doctors and medical specialists as soon as possible!*

"COMPARED TO BIPOLAR'S MAGIC, REALITY SEEMS A RAW DEAL. IT'S NOT JUST THE BOREDOM THAT MAKES RECOVERY SO DIFFICULT, IT'S THE SLOW DAWNING PAIN THAT COMES WITH SANITY – THE REALIZATION OF ILLNESS, THE HUMILIATING SCENES, THE BLOWN MONEY AND FRIENDSHIPS, AND CONFIDENCE. DEPRESSION SEEMS ALMOST INEVITABLE."

– DAVID LOVELACE

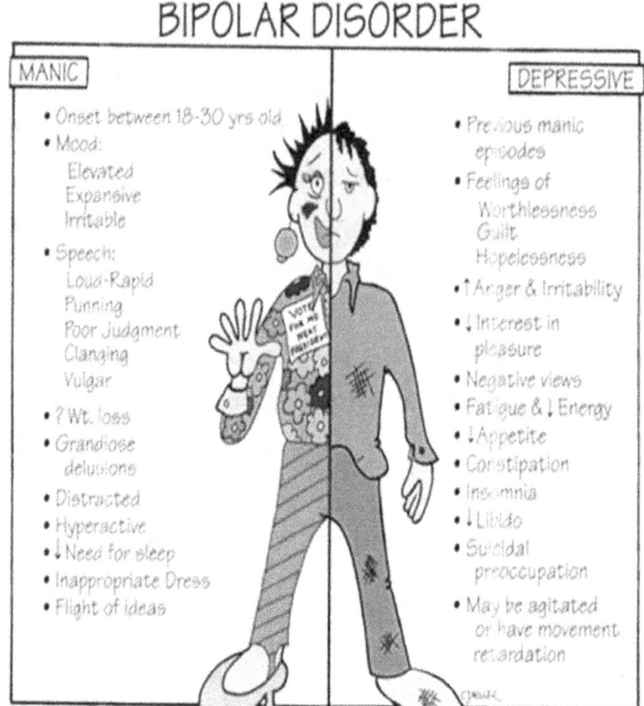

Table Of Contents

**It is the goal of this guide to provide you the reader with a unique blend of self-help and first-person accounts from people who live with bipolar disorder on a daily basis.**

For those who have been given a diagnosis of a life-threatening illness or a chronic, debilitating illness face an overwhelming number of challenges during treatment and throughout their entire lives, on a physical, emotional, social, spiritual, and financial level.

In an effort to breakdown the real-life issues of bipolar, told in the words of the bipolar sufferers, we hope that we can help you better understand this illness.

We hope this layman's terms approach will assist readers in placing themselves in the position of a person with bipolar disorder.

To aids readers in comprehending the consequences of severe mood swings, helplessness, and cognitive distortions.

The commonality of the experiences described in these essays is what binds them together and lends a human dimension to a condition that can be quite terrifying.

True accounts that will give you courage, solace, and strength.

*Marcella Gucci*

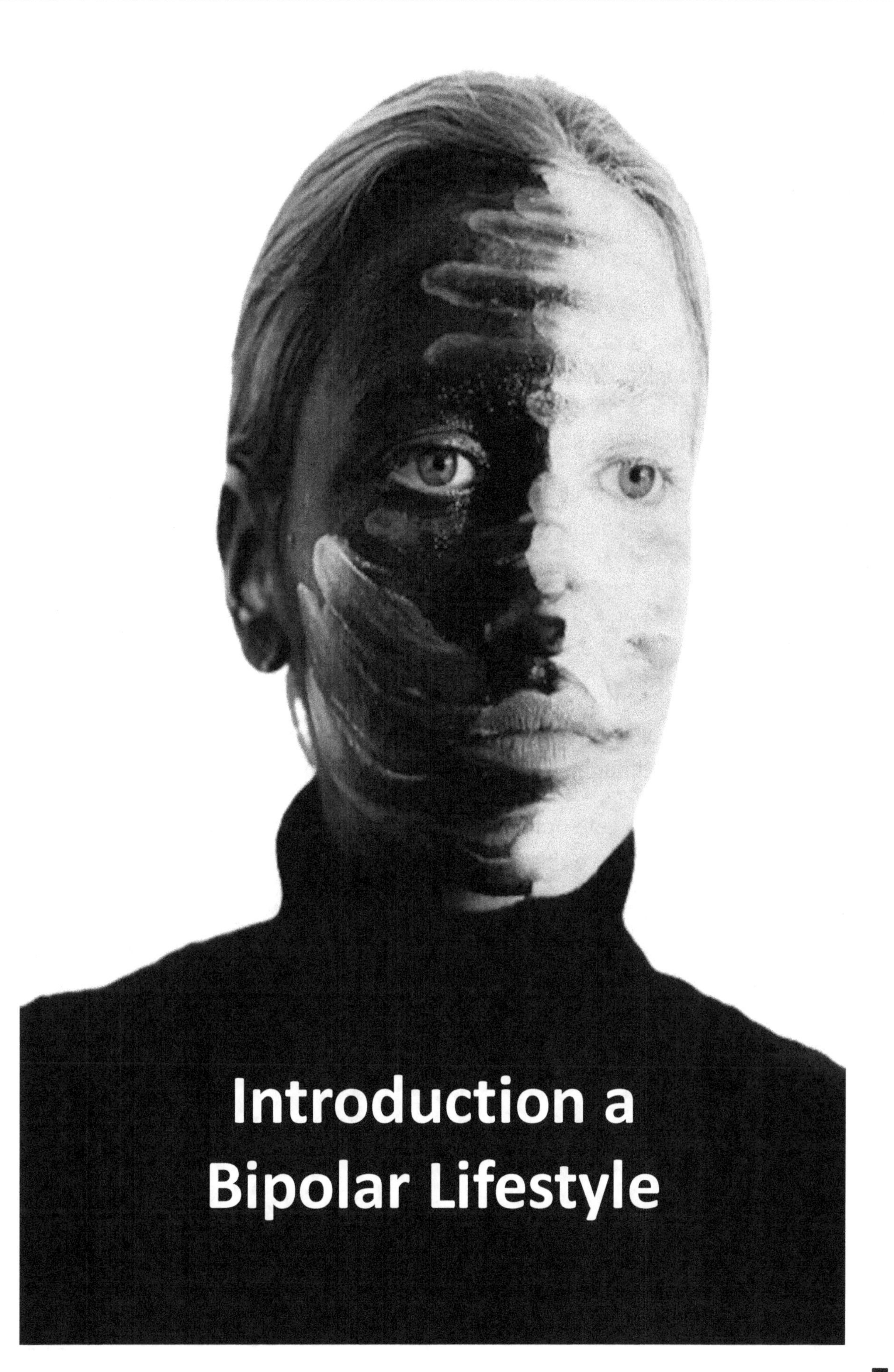

Introduction a
Bipolar Lifestyle

## Bipolar Disorder in Real Life

Always remember that, while bipolar disorder behavior can be irritating and damaging, it is not intended to punish you or anyone else. Compassion goes a long way when someone is experiencing a mood fluctuation. It is beneficial to keep this in mind.

Bipolar disorder is not a problem that can be solved overnight.  It's easy to be hopeful and thrilled about something new, but when things get difficult (or your spouse doesn't respond right away), it's tempting to fall back into old habits in which you must do everything to keep your relationship together.

Perhaps your partner is too sick to reply. If this is the case, or if your spouse is under great stress or has warped thinking, they may be unable to complete the necessary tasks.

This will naturally irritate you. However, you are not alone. Many bipolar disorder spouses must undertake the work on their own at first.

It can be extremely exhausting for both spouses, and it can be difficult to find support. The spouse with bipolar disorder may have intense ups and downs. This can be both extremely challenging and stressful to live with.

It can also be difficult to get support from friends and family in the same way as someone who does not have the disorder.

If you are the spouse with the diagnosis, you may experience isolation, shame, and guilt from your own thoughts and feelings as well as from how your behavior affects your partner.

You may also feel like you can't be vulnerable and ask for help because you don't want to be a burden.

While it's important to practice self-care, you don't want your disorder to affect your partner or your relationship.

# Introduction a Bipolar Lifestyle

**How we managed as a family:**

"Though Percy was the one experiencing symptoms, the impact of bipolar disorder was felt by the entire family."

"His depression was sad and painful to watch, and we were terrified when his mood changed to manic," the author recalls.

We incorrectly attributed his extreme mood swings to the strength of his personality.
I believe he would have sought appropriate medical care and been accurately diagnosed much sooner if he had realized his moods and behavior were symptoms of a chemical imbalance that could be treated

Percy perfectly illustrates how the road to recovery begins with listening, communicating empathically, and recognizing symptoms.

Percy wants families dealing with bipolar disorder to know that there is hope with the right diagnosis and treatment.

**One day at a time:**

Rather than worrying about how you will get through the rest of the week or the coming month, try to concentrate on today.

Every day can present us with new opportunities to learn new things, including how to deal with problems.

Concentrate on the present moment and stop speculating about what might happen next week. The following week will take care of itself.

A good way to deal with your fear is to counteract your negative thoughts with positive statements and realistic thinking.

When you have scary or worrying thoughts, try to get rid of them by asking yourself questions that will help you stay objective and logical.

# Introduction a Bipolar Lifestyle

We may become nervous when performing a frightening task.

When this happens, imagine yourself performing the task.

For example, you and your team must play in the championship hockey game in front of a large crowd in the coming days. Before the big day arrives, visualize yourself playing the game.

Assume you're performing in front of a large crowd. You will be better prepared to perform for real if you play the game in your head.

Self-visualization is a great way to reduce anxiety and stress when something bad is about to happen. (see section on Visualize your affirmations)

**Do-It-Yourself Bipolar Disorder Prevention.**
It makes no difference if you have already been diagnosed with bipolar disorder type one or two, or if you have been battling it for some time.

What matters is that you have complete control over the situation you're in. There is no one else who can work it all out unless you decide to get better on your own. You are the only person who can assist yourself.

There are also resources available, such as support from family and friends, mental institutions and facilities, and so on.

However, aside from those support systems that are readily available to lend a hand, you can do it on your own.

**How? Here are some suggestions.**

1.  Be informed. You must read more and more about what you are experiencing in order to gain a better understanding of the illness that you are suffering from.
    - Knowledge is an important factor to keep in mind as you learn about the disorder's facts.
    - You can also teach your family so that if any unusual activities occur, they will know what to do. It is also a good idea to consult with your doctor about your preferences.

# Introduction a Bipolar Lifestyle

2.  Restore normalcy.
    - Do not let your disorder prevent you from performing routine tasks.
    - It is critical that you allow yourself to overcome the disease rather than be overcome by it.
    - Your daily routines, such as doing chores, working, walking your dog, and sleeping at least six to eight hours a day, can help you forget you are bipolar. Exercise is another way that the body can move around negative energy, such as stress.

3.  Always take medications exactly as directed.
    - Because bipolar disorder is a recurring disorder, you can not stop it unless your doctor tells you to.
    - You must take your medications as prescribed by your doctor.
    - Even if you are feeling better or have no signs of manic or depressive episodes, antidepressants and mood stabilizers should be taken on a daily basis.
    - If there are signs of side effects and you can no longer tolerate it, notify your doctor immediately so that he can suggest other alternatives or reduce the drug's dosage.

4.  Get rid of stressors and stimulants.
    - It is critical that you avoid factors that may contribute to the onset of your disorder.
    - Avoid people and situations that will cause you to become positively or negatively hyper.
    - This may agitate you or aggravate your current behavior. Stimulants include nicotine (cigarette smoking), caffeine (coffee, sodas, and chocolates), and other substances that can cause your condition to be stimulated.
    - These can also cause insomnia.

5.  Give up drinking alcohol.
    - This is one of the most prudent things you can do to safeguard yourself against behavioral occurrences.
    - Alcohol is a natural depressant, and increased consumption may exacerbate your condition.
    - Also, alcohol cancels out the effects of your medicines and can change how they work, which could hurt your liver and cause other health problems.

# Introduction a Bipolar Lifestyle

## Tips for Staying Married When Your Partner Has Bipolar Disorder

Create a support system.

- It's important to have people around you who you can lean on when you and your partner need support.
- This can include family and friends, a therapist, or a support group of people who are also struggling with a partner who has bipolar disorder.
- Having a support system can help keep you accountable and on track with self-care when your partner needs extra support.

Set boundaries.

- You don't have to do everything for your partner or be everything for him or her.
- You don't have to be responsible for your partner's actions or decisions.
- You have the right to set boundaries and encourage your partner to take responsibility for their own actions.

Don't let your relationship become toxic.

- If you and your partner are feeling overwhelmed, it's important to take a step back and figure out what needs to change.
- This could mean taking time apart to reset, seeing a therapist as a couple or individually, or finding a support group for people who are in relationships with people with bipolar disorder.

My husband's illness doesn't define him – it shows him in his most authentic form: when he's happy or sad. It shows me how much he loves and cares about me no matter what happens inside his head.

So when people ask me what my husband's diagnosis means to me - especially if they are family members who don't understand - I explain it as an opportunity for them to spend more time with a happy spouse who is also capable of loving and caring for them at the same time.

It's important to be open and honest with each other about how it affects you both and to find ways to support each other.

It's also important to take care of oneself so you don't become exhausted and resentful while staying supportive of your partner.

It can be helpful to find other people going through the same thing and to seek professional help if needed.

# Introduction a Bipolar Lifestyle

## Tips for Staying Married When Your Partner Has Bipolar Disorder

There are many things that you can do to help your husband get better.

You can support him while he is still taking care of himself, and you can offer words of encouragement when he is feeling down.

You can also help him by being open and honest about his condition with him.

You can also make sure that he has access to mental health resources like therapy and medication.

Even though your husband may seem quite normal, it's important to remain aware of the fact that he could flip at any second.

When he's in the grips of mania, your husband can be impulsive, he can make bad choices, and he can sometimes forget things that he should definitely remember!

Because of these things, your husband could accidentally hurt himself or another person.

It's also possible that your husband could be in a deep depression where he doesn't feel like he can get through to anyone and doesn't want to talk about it.

Again, this is a very difficult condition to manage on your own. Depression is a serious disease and can't be overcome by will power or by making small talk.

This means you and your husband have to spend a lot of time talking to get through it together.

Your partner may end up being much quieter and less talkative when he's in a depressed state compared to when he's in a manic state.

When he's in a depressed state, he might even become more withdrawn and shy, which can make him less attractive to other people. But when he's in a manic state, he might say or do things that are actually helpful, like helping out a family member or coworkers who is in need.

It might also be worth remembering that your partner doesn't always have to be in control of his moods. You can always take a deep breath and try to be patient with your partner while he works through his issues.

# Introduction a Bipolar Lifestyle

## Tips for Staying Married When Your Partner Has Bipolar Disorder

People with bipolar disorder are people, not just the disorder. So, while it's important to get to know the signs and symptoms of the disorder, it's just as important to get to know the person behind the diagnosis.

People with bipolar disorder are complex and difficult to understand. The best way to survive in their world is to be open-minded and accepting of everyone around you.

This means you can have an open mind about your partner's illness, but you also need to be realistic about the chances of him or her having a mood swing.

**A symptom of bipolar disorder is hypersexuality.**
This is the big one! People with Bipolar I Disorder have very high rates of hypersexuality symptom.

Like with all the other symptoms of Bipolar I, you can Peak levels of hypersexuality are associated with very high risks of developing full blown intimacy issues, substance use, and even self-destructive habits.

**How to recognize bipolar hypersexuality.**
This is where it gets a little harder. Because not everyone with bipolar will experience sexual side effects to the same degree.

While people with Bipolar I Disorder usually have quite high rates of sexual side effects, people with Bipolar II Disorder are much less likely to experience the same side effects.

Here's where the manual for the Bipolar II Diagnostic and Statistical Manual (Bipolar II DSM) comes in handy.

The DSM defines sexual side effects as: 'A change in behavior, a change in mood, or both, which is a result of sexual interactions (e.g., an increased sex drive) or which may be the result of a sexual interaction (e.g., increased orgasm).

**Introduction a Bipolar Lifestyle**

15

## Tips for Staying Married When Your Partner Has Bipolar Disorder

Some symptoms that may indicate hypersexuality in a person with Bipolar II Disorder include:

- Excessive (or unusual) interest in sex Increased or decreased sexual desire or behavior Increased frequency of sex or sexual activity
- Over masturbation Extreme porn use

**The manic side of hypersexuality**
Even though most people with Bipolar II Disorder don't experience the same extreme levels of sexual side effects as people with Bipolar I Disorder, there's no question that the lows are just as, if not more, devastating.

A person's 'manic' phase of bipolar disorder is often times more intense than their 'depressive' phase. This is especially true for people with obsessions about sex.

These levels of sexual intensity can last years, or be brief affairs. They can also be sparked by a single event, such as a breakup, or being scorned.

A person's sexual behavior can also change suddenly, and unexpectedly, during a Bipolar II manic episode.

**How to deal with hypersexuality in bipolar**
The most important thing you can do for your partner is be there for them.

This means actively listening to what your partner is trying to say, even when they're trying to say it in ways that are hard to understand.

When you can't communicate well, or when communication isn't possible, you have to spend time apart from your partner.

This can be hard, but it's the only way to protect both of you from the damage caused by sexual side effects.

It can also protect your relationship from falling apart at any time.

# Introduction a Bipolar Lifestyle

## Understanding Suicidal Tendencies Within the Context of Bipolar Disorder

Before we get into the details, let's take a step back and look at the main reasons why people with bipolar disorder kill themselves.

Generally speaking, there are two forms of bipolar disorder: bipolar I and bipolar II. These two groups can be thought of as symptoms that can be used to figure out what's wrong.

- In Bipolar Disorder Type I, the person may have at least one or two manic episodes, even though they haven't had any depressive episodes before.

- Bipolar Disorder Type II - The person must have at least one bout of depression and at least one bout of hypomania.
    - Hypomanic episodes are usually not as bad and last a lot less time than manic episodes, which usually only last a few days and are not very bad.
    - Hypomanic episodes are marked by irritation and problems with normal functioning that don't need to be treated in the hospital.

- Cyclothymia: - This is included in the category, but is considered the milder form of bipolar disorder.
    - Compared to the extremes seen by those with bipolar disorder, cyclothymic mood fluctuations are modest.

- Psychosis: - This is when bipolar disorder becomes severe. The individual experiences delusional and hallucinatory moments that remove them from reality.
    - Some individuals mistakenly believe they are someone else or perceive things that are not present.

With everything associated with the disease, only one thing remains: suicide.

Because the individual can no longer comprehend what is happening to him, his behavior now dominates his entire system and his thoughts and emotions.

So, a person commits suicide when he or she thinks he or she can't do anything good.

# Introduction a Bipolar Lifestyle

Suicide becomes one of the most successful means of evading every difficulty that might arise in a person's life.

If someone in the family has already been diagnosed with the condition, it makes sense for everyone in the family to get tested.

Ensure that the individual is cared for, any suicidal intentions must be addressed immediately in order to rule out idealism.

It is recommended that the individual get medical attention.

The suicidal risk will manifest earlier in the illness' progression.

To figure out if someone has suicidal thoughts, you need to look at the following signs and symptoms:
- Hopelessness and helplessness
- Thoughts about dying or discussions of the afterlife
- Considers himself or herself a burden to his or her family and friends.
- Abuse of alcohol and illicit drugs
- Creating random farewell notes
- Organizing one's affairs in preparation for imminent death
- It is possible to kill yourself, especially if you are in the early stages of bipolar disorder.

Bipolar or not, if you or someone you know is feeling suicidal, you should always find ways to get rid of it, such as calling a doctor for advice, never leaving suicidal people alone, and removing any means of self-harm from the person's reach.

To completely eliminate the risk of suicidal ideation, it is crucial to comprehend the underlying reasons of the condition.

Life is the most important thing that must be protected. It's unfortunate that it was wasted.

# The Good, the Bad, and the Ugly of Bipolar Disorder in Relationships

**The Good, the Bad, and the Ugly of Bipolar Disorder in Relationships**

If you have a mental health condition, you might be unsure of whether to discuss it with your significant other. And if you're single, you might wonder whether dating is out for you because of your mental health issue.

It's crucial to understand that many people who suffer from severe mental illnesses have committed, enduring relationships.

While a bad relationship can exacerbate your symptoms, especially in cases of depression, a good relationship offers valuable social support during trying times.

There are three types of bipolar disorder in relationships: positive, negative, and ugly.

Here are some of the good things that can come from being in a relationship with someone who has bipolar disorder:

1. They may be more spontaneous and fun than other partners.
2. They understand your ups and downs and can offer support during tough times.
3. They can help you stay balanced by providing stability.
4. They may be more creative than other partners and can help you see the world in a different way.
5. They understand your need for space and alone time.
6. They can help you learn more about yourself.
7. They can teach you how to accept yourself.
8. You will never get bored when it comes to sex because they're always up for trying new things!
9. They will always be honest with their thoughts and feelings, which might lead to some intense conversations but could also mean they won't stray outside of the relationship or cheat on you (as long as their honesty doesn't lead to anger or resentment).
10. Your family will likely accept them more readily since people know what bipolar disorder is nowadays and tend not judge as harshly as before (unlike years ago).
11. You'll often find them giving back to the community and making an effort to help others, either through donations or volunteering.
12. You'll often find them having a positive outlook on life, even if they don't feel great at any given moment due to symptoms of depression or mania.
13. They won't let the relationship stagnate; they make sure you both work towards meeting each other's needs and desires, even if this means one partner takes care of themselves first sometimes (just like taking care of yourself first sometimes is important for self-care!).

## The Good, the Bad, and the Ugly of Bipolar Disorder in Relationships

14. It can be refreshing to date someone who knows that mental illness isn't all in your head--especially when there are so many misconceptions out there.
15. There's a greater understanding of mental illness among society today and we're finally breaking down barriers and stigma (thanks to celebrities openly discussing their struggles) so dating someone with bipolar disorder shouldn't seem like such a big deal anymore.
16. Even though mental illnesses require ongoing maintenance, maintaining a relationship requires ongoing maintenance too! And just because you love somebody with bipolar disorder doesn't mean you're letting them off the hook for treating themselves well too--you still encourage healthy habits just as much as any other partner would too!
17. For those who date someone with bipolar disorder, you can make a difference in their lives and provide hope to those who are struggling.
18. They often listen better than most partners and take what you say seriously.
19. Bipolar disorder is not contagious.
20. Dating someone with bipolar disorder teaches us compassion and empathy for those living with mental illness--not pity or disdain (I'm looking at you, Hollywood)!
21. You'll always have something to talk about because mental health is so prevalent these days and awareness around the subject is growing!

**The Bad ( The Negative)**

Bipolar disorder can be a real challenge in relationships. Those of us who live with bipolar know that our moods can sometimes be unpredictable and extreme. We may feel on top of the world one day and then sink into a deep depression the next. This roller coaster ride can be tough for both us and our partners. It's often difficult to figure out how to help each other through these ups and downs. If you have bipolar disorder, here are some tips for handling your mood swings:

1. Be aware of triggers. What events lead to your mood swings? Pay attention so you can start to identify patterns. For example, if you have hypomania and your partner has just left home without telling you where he is going, this might set off an episode of mania.
2. Try not to push people away when they try to help you – it's often hard enough just being yourself when living with bipolar! Remember that they want what's best for you too.

3) Talk to your partner about how to communicate when you feel a mood swing coming on.
   - For example, if you have mania and feel your partner is taking advantage of your elevated mood, let him or her know what you need.
   - Maybe you need some alone time;
   - or maybe it would be helpful to talk through options for cutting back on spending money.
4) Ask for support from friends and family. Sometimes we can't see clearly during a mood swing.
   - Asking for advice from people who know us well can help keep you on track with your treatment plan.
   - If you don't feel safe doing that with someone at home, call a trusted friend or a hotline to talk through things.

**The Ugly**

Bipolar disorder can be a tough illness to deal with in any relationship. It can cause problems with communication, trust, and commitment. It can also lead to infidelity and financial problems.

If you're in a relationship with someone who has bipolar disorder, it's important to be understanding and patient. You also need to be honest with yourself about whether or not you're willing to deal with the challenges that come along with the illness.

For some people, this is too much of a burden and they decide to end the relationship. For others, they are able to work through their differences and create an even stronger bond.

However, when both partners have bipolar disorder then they will likely understand each other better because they share similar experiences which helps them develop compassion for one another. Even if things don't work out between two people who have the same diagnosis, it doesn't mean that they won't remain friends and support each other in dealing with their illness.

When one partner has bipolar disorder and the other does not, it can sometimes result in resentment from the person without the condition.

**The Good, the Bad, and the Ugly of Bipolar Disorder in Relationships**

Finding the right person to spend your life with will take time and patience - just like everything else in life! It may seem impossible now, but as soon as you meet that special someone, you'll know that it was worth the wait.

Here, we go over a few of the inquiries into romantic relationships that people with mental health issues make.

**Should I Tell My Partner that I am bipolar and when?**

You should tell your partner that you are bipolar as soon as possible. It is important to be open and honest with the person you are in a relationship with. If you are not comfortable telling your partner, you can tell a close friend or family member who can help support you. There are also many resources available online or through mental health professionals.

What if my partner doesn't want to be with me anymore?

- If your partner decides they do not want to be with you after you have disclosed your bipolar disorder, it is not your fault. It is important to remember that you cannot control how someone else feels.
- You can reach out to a mental health professional or support group for help dealing with this difficult situation.
- Do not feel guilty about the decision made by your partner- remember, there are other people who will accept you for all of who you are.

**How Should I Explain My Mental Health Condition to My Partner?**

It can be difficult to explain a mental health condition to a partner. You may feel like you need to protect them from the negative aspects of your condition or that they won't be able to understand.

However, it is important to be open and honest with your partner about your mental health. This will help them to understand you better and provide support.

## The Good, the Bad, and the Ugly of Bipolar Disorder in Relationships

There are a few things you should keep in mind when explaining your mental health condition to your partner:

1. Be open and honest about what you're experiencing.
2. Avoid using negative words to describe yourself or your condition.
3. Be patient if they don't understand immediately.
4. Offer resources for further reading or understanding.
5. Have patience and compassion for your partner as they process the information.
6. Keep trying! Your relationship may not improve overnight but there are steps you can take to build trust and understanding in your relationship while supporting each other through mental illness.

**The complicated issue of sex and hypersexual behavior in Bipolar.**

When it comes to sex and bipolar disorder, there are a lot of myths and misconceptions.

For example, some people think that people with bipolar disorder are always hypersexual, or that they can't be in a committed relationship. However, the reality is much more complicated. While some people with bipolar disorder may experience periods of hypersexuality, others may go through periods of sexual indifference.

Some people with bipolar disorder also feel guilty about their hypersexual behavior and either try to stop themselves from engaging in these behaviors, or avoid romantic relationships altogether.

Those who do pursue relationships often find themselves struggling to balance the highs and lows of their moods while juggling the needs of their partner. In the event that someone does act on feelings of hypersexuality, guilt becomes an issue as well.

**All this begs the question: Can you have a happy, healthy relationship if you have bipolar disorder?**

In short-term studies conducted by researcher Dr. Tiihonen and his colleagues at Helsinki University Hospital, researchers found that people with bipolar disorder were not more likely to have marital problems than those without mental illness.

## The Good, the Bad, and the Ugly of Bipolar Disorder in Relationships

Dr. Tiihonen theorizes that because marriage provides both partners with emotional support and social structure which can help offset negative symptoms associated with mental illness, marriages actually improve quality of life for those diagnosed with bipolar disorder.

**But what happens when one person has manic episodes during which he or she becomes hypersexual?**

It's important to note that hypersexual means different things to different people.
- A woman might consider herself hypersexual because she masturbates five times a day;
- meanwhile, her husband might consider himself hypersexual because he only masturbates once every few days.
- What one couple considers completely normal could be considered completely abnormal by another couple - and vice versa.

Hypersexuality presents a unique challenge for couples:

Many couples will agree beforehand that sex is something they do together, not separately; but when one person starts acting out sexually (either positively or negatively), the other partner may become resentful and hurt.

There's no easy answer to how best to deal with such scenarios - but talking openly about expectations seems like a good start!

The tricky thing about dating someone with bipolar disorder is that, unlike many other illnesses, we don't know whether our partner will live with us a lifetime or just until next year.

We also don't know whether our partner will spend all their time as high mania or deep depression. And since we don't know, we must rely on what they tell us.

As I've already said, sex doesn't seem to be much of an issue for people living with Bipolar II Disorder.

One of the most important issues is that people with bipolar disorder may struggle to form and maintain a connection with their partner.

## The Good, the Bad, and the Ugly of Bipolar Disorder in Relationships

During periods of depressive episodes, they may be too numb to engage in any kind of sexual activity, or they may even want to actively repel their partner.

When they're in a manic episode, they may come on too strong and overwhelm their partner.

Additionally, some people with bipolar disorder abuse substances, including alcohol and drugs.

This makes it difficult for them to communicate their desires clearly and sets the stage for unintentional boundary crossings.

If a partner with bipolar disorder abuses substances then tries to initiate sex when sober, he or she may come across as insensitive or uncaring because the partner may be confused by the sudden change in interest levels.

**What about sex when you have bipolar disorder?**

In a study of people with bipolar disorder, Dr. Kupka and his colleagues found that people with bipolar disorder were not more likely to have higher rates of sexual dysfunction than those without mental illness.

They also reported less frequent sexual intercourse, which they say may be due to the presence of fatigue, low self-esteem, or difficulties in concentration.

This finding is supported by a recent review on sexuality and bipolar disorder by Ms. Gondolf and her colleagues in the Journal of Clinical Psychiatry which concluded that sexual dysfunction is a common symptom among persons with  disorders.

Sexuality is an extremely sensitive topic for anyone struggling with mental illness because sex is often a way we learn about ourselves and connect with others.

For those of us who are neurodivergent, sexuality can be a vital tool for exploring our gender identity and building a sense of sexual agency.

Sexual expression may also be one of the last remaining outlets for creativity left when other areas of life are feeling restrictive or uncomfortable.

# The Good, the Bad, and the Ugly of Bipolar Disorder in Relationships

**The relationship between sexual dysfunction and bipolar disorder**

It's no secret that bipolar disorder can wreak havoc on your life. But did you know that it can also affect your sex life?

According to a recent study, nearly 60 percent of people with bipolar disorder experience some form of sexual dysfunction.
- Among men, this includes erectile dysfunction or problems ejaculating.
- Among women, it may be vaginal dryness or pain during intercourse.

**How do most relationships end up with bipolar?**

Most relationships end up with bipolar when one person ends up feeling neglected or unsupported.

It can be difficult to deal with the constant mood swings and emotional ups and downs that come with the disorder.

If you're in a relationship with someone who has bipolar disorder, it's important to be supportive and understanding. However, it's also important to set boundaries.

Otherwise, the relationship can become too chaotic.

A partner needs to have their own space and independence. You need your own time for activities as well.

Trying new things on your own will allow you to maintain a sense of self and not get sucked into the other person's world of moods, which is sometimes hard for people with bipolar to manage themselves.

**What about kids?**

When couples have children together, the risks increase significantly because kids are vulnerable to the moods of parents and grandparents.

## The Good, the Bad, and the Ugly of Bipolar Disorder in Relationships

If your partner has bipolar disorder, it might help if you talk about parenting strategies ahead of time so that both parents are on board with how they'll handle things like discipline, chores, bedtime routines etcetera.

Parents should also make sure that kids understand why dad or mommy isn't always happy, sad, angry, or anxious - but they are still loved.

Kids often feel guilty and think they've done something wrong when mommy gets mad at them.

Parents should reassure them that mommy is just sad and frustrated sometimes.

 Make sure you model healthy coping skills for the children by practicing them yourself - especially during tough times.

For example, you might try some deep breathing exercises to calm down before an argument, take a walk outside when feeling restless, and do some yoga to relax. These are all tools that may help reduce stress.

As adults we need this more than ever because of the extra responsibilities we carry every day.

It's never easy being in a relationship with someone who has bipolar disorder - but it can be worth it!

That said, partners should work to create a mutually-beneficial partnership where everyone feels supported and loved.

It doesn't matter if your partner has bipolar disorder or not - healthy partnerships require work from both partners.

# What To Do When Your Parents Or Siblings Suffer From Bipolar Disorder.

**What To Do When Your Parents Or Siblings Suffer From Bipolar Disorder**.

People with bipolar disorder and their loved ones often face challenges that are unique to them.

For some, symptoms tend to develop over time, while others experience a rapid mood swing. Regardless of how the person's illness manifests itself, one thing is for sure — dealing with bipolar disorder as a family member or a close friend is no easy feat.

Whether you're the patient who's been diagnosed, or a family member or friend of someone who has been referred to a psychiatrist for evaluation, treatment planning, and more than anything else – understanding what exactly your loved one is going through can feel like the most overwhelming task.

**Bipolar disorder in a family member or friend**

In some cases, you're the family member or friend who has a loved one with bipolar disorder. In other cases, you're the person who has the illness themselves. bipolar disorder in a family member or friend, like any other illness, is nothing short of a medical emergency.

If you or your loved one is experiencing any of the following signs, it is crucial that you get medical help right away:

- Depressed mood
- Feeling of hopelessness
- Sleepiness or inability to stay awake
- Change in appetite
- Change in their sex life
- Suicidal thoughts

If you or your loved one is displaying any of these symptoms, it's vital that you get help as soon as possible. Not only will treatment help your loved one get the better of their illness, but it will also help put your own health back on track.

**What to do when your parent or sibling suffers from bipolar disorder**

There are a number of things you can do when you're the parent or a close relative of someone who has bipolar disorder. The first step is to understand the disorder better, so you can better appreciate the unique symptoms and trajectory your loved one is on.

Once you've got the broad strokes of the disorder, the next step is to get to know your loved one better. Ask them how they're doing all the time, and pay attention to the details. Make an effort to get to know your loved one's habits, triggers, and their daily life. This will help you to better understand your loved one and what they go through on a day-to-day basis.

**How to identify bipolar disorder in a loved one**

While there are many ways to tell if your loved one has bipolar disorder, the following four signs are the most common:

- Changes in mood: rapid, extreme, or bizarre
- Changes in appetite: increased or decreased
- Changes in their behavior: irritability, impulsivity, or unusual activity
- Changes in their work or school performance

You may notice that your loved one's moods change from time to time, and that's perfectly normal.

**How to help a family member or friend who has bipolar disorder.**

Despite the challenges and stigma attached to it, *bipolar disorder cannot be cured.* However, there are a number of ways to help your loved one with this illness.

Talk to them about their feelings. Moods and feelings are intertwined, so even though your loved one may not be able to control their feelings, you can still communicate with them and learn from them.

Try to remain open-minded about what your loved one's feelings might be. - Don't over analyze things.

Having a grand theory about what's going on in your loved one's head may be Sandbox of Dora-worthy, but it will do nothing but stress your loved one out.

**Be there for them.**
The people around you will affect how you feel, so make an effort to connect with those around you. Your loved one needs you more than they need themselves.

Know the difference between antidepressants and antipsychotics. While both medications can help with the symptoms of bipolar disorder, one medication may provide a greater range of effects than the other, and therefore has a greater chance of helping your loved one.

**Pay attention to your own symptoms.**

Many people with bipolar disorder experience major mood swings between the " extremes " of mania and depression. Pay attention to what you're feeling, and don't ignore your own feelings unless you're in a state of shock or anxiety.

**Don't take anything for granted.**

Your loved one may not be able to take certain medications or have a certain mood swing that you're experiencing. Ensure that you're aware of what's available to you, and understand that your loved one's condition may progress in ways you aren't expecting.

Don't isolate yourself. Being alone can cause major mood swings, so spending time with others can help you out a lot.

Don't put down the phone. Even if you think you're not in danger of being overheard, the last thing you want to do is put your loved one on the phone when they're in distress.

Take your time and consider how to best handle a situation before speaking to a person on the phone.

Don't be afraid to ask for help. Sometimes you have to ask for help, and when you don't, things can get very difficult for you and your loved one.

Don't be afraid to contact a therapist or mental health professional. Mental health treatment is very effective, and often accessible.

And don't forget to take your medication. You don't have to take the medicine for the entire time your loved one has the disorder, or for the entirety of your relationship.

**The symptoms of bipolar disorder**

You might have thought that your loved one's mood swings were due to the illness, but that's not the case.

Bipolar disorder is a brain condition that affects people in different ways. It can either be an acute condition, where someone has a manic episode and then becomes depressed, or a chronic condition, where someone has two moods and then becomes manic again.

**Symptoms of bipolar disorder include:**

- **Mania:** a rapid and persistent increase in behavior, talk, and activities
- **Depression**: a low mood that lasts longer than two weeks
- **Mania-Depression:** a state in which someone has two moods and becomes manic again. This may be sudden, unexpected shifts in energy and interest that last for a few hours or a few days.
- **Fantasized about death or self-harm.** When one part of you wants to commit suicide and another wants to stay alive, things can get very scary. Impulsive and sometimes reckless.
- You might say your loved one is *"all over the place"* when it comes to decision-making.
- **Lack of focus and clings to routines.** Bipolar illness is often characterized by poor focus, a lack of initiative, and a need to cling to routines and follow established paths even when feelings are hurt or needed to be different.

It is important to remember that these are descriptions of how someone with bipolar disorder might behave, rather than how someone with bipolar disorder actually is.

**What to do when your loved one has bipolar disorder**

People with bipolar disorder often show features that are unique to the illness. For example, one person may have extreme moods, while another may be calm and reserved.

Your loved one may also have a specific way of talking or behaving that you'd never notice unless you looked for it. To get the most out of your loved one, you'll want to pay attention to what they're doing, saying, and experiencing.

**Asking yourself:**

- What am I doing or saying that I should be paying attention to?
- Is there something I'm not doing or saying that I should be looking out for?
- Am I experiencing any unusual changes in my life that I'm not noticing?

**Bottom line**

Bipolar disorder is a chronic condition that messes with your brain's chemistry. It's often misdiagnosed as something else, so it's important to know what to look for and how to identify it.

The good news is that getting help for your loved one doesn't have to be a difficult or scary process.

The hard work starts when you decide to talk to your doctor or mental health professional about your concerns.

The good news is that getting help for your loved one doesn't have to be a difficult or scary process.

# BIPOLAR DISORDER

Bipolar disorder (BPD), previously known as manic depression, is a mental disorder that causes periods of depression and periods of abnormally elevated mood (is known as mania).

The causes are not clearly understood, but both environmental and genetic factors play a role. Environmental risk factors include a history of childhood abuse and long-term stress.

## SOME SYMPTOMS

- ✓ Uncharacteristic periods of anger and aggression.
- ✓ Grandiosity and overconfidence.
- ✓ Easy tearfulness, frequent sadness.
- ✓ Needing little sleep to feel rested.
- ✓ Uncharacteristic impulsive behavior.
- ✓ Moodiness.
- ✓ Confusion and inattention.

## THE KEYS TO SELF-HELP

Get educated 

Get moving 

Keep stress in check 

Seek support 

Stay closely to friends and family 

Sleep and eat healthy 

Monitor your moods 

# Bipolar in Teens - What to Know and How to Help

While adult Bipolar Disorder is usually treated with medications, many teens who suffer from the condition find it difficult to control their moods and stay on the right side of reality.

Bipolar disorder can strike at any age, but often strikes in adolescence and early adulthood. There are several signs that a teen may have the condition, but the symptoms most commonly seen among teens are similar to those seen in adults.

Therefore, knowing what to look for and how to help a teen affected by bipolar disorder is just as important as diagnosing the disease.

The following information will help you better understand how to help a teen with bipolar disorder. As the medical community continues to understand the condition better, we will develop better and more accurate diagnostic criteria. Therefore, the information provided here may evolve over time.

Reading this article may also provide you with some insight into the way your child thinks and processes information. Understanding how your child thinks may help you better identify areas of confusion and strengths that your child does show.

Knowing this may also help you identify areas of strength and enable you to better guide your child's thinking.

**What Is the Difference Between Adult Bipolar Disorder and Teens Bipolar Disorder?**

Adolescents and young adults are often in a state of high emotion, and they may not be able to control this emotion.

This makes them particularly vulnerable to the impact of mood changes on their behavior, relationships, and mental health.

It may be that your teenager's mood shifts are different from yours, or that they are in a more volatile state than you.

# Bipolar in Teens - What to Know and How to Help

As a parent, you may want to understand why this is the case so that you can help your child be as poor treatment free as possible.

One of the first signs of a mood change in an adolescent is a change in social habits.

These may include changes in friends, school, and interests.

It is possible for a teenager to remain very close to friends and also to experience changes in social habits. A change in friends, in contrast, is much less common.

**How Is Bipolar Disorder in Teens Diagnosed?**

The two main types of Bipolar Disorder in teens are manic-depressive and mixed.

A diagnosis of mixed Bipolar Disorder is not as accurate as a diagnosis of manic-depressive Bipolar Disorder because it includes symptoms from both mania and depression.

However, the symptoms of both types of Bipolar Disorder can be observed in adolescents, making a diagnosis a bit more difficult.

In addition to the above, if a teen:

- Has had a history of mood altering substances, such as risky sexual behaviors,
- Substance use disorders,
- Family history of mood-altering substance use,

It may be necessary to rule out the possibility of a more general medical condition, such as a mental illness or drug or alcohol dependency.

Additionally, a thorough health history should be taken, including medical and surgical history.

**What Is the Treatment for Bipolar Disorder in Teens?**

When a teen has Bipolar Disorder, the first step is to get a complete medical evaluation.

# Bipolar in Teens - What to Know and How to Help

This will help the doctor to better understand the cause of the teenager's mood changes and will allow the doctor to better treat the patient.

Treatment can vary depending on a number of factors, including the nature and severity of the teen's symptoms, the patient's age, and the patient's physical and emotional health.

Unfortunately, there are no medications that can treat Bipolar Disorder in teens.

Most adolescents with the condition will need some form of support as they deal with their moods. These may include therapy, medication, and/or self-help groups.

## Key Takeaway

Bipolar disorder can strike at any age, but often strikes in the teens and young adulthood.

The symptoms are similar to those seen in adults, so it's important to know what to look for and how to help a teen with Bipolar disorder.

If you think your child may have bipolar disorder, or is worried that they may have the condition, organize to see a medical specialist as soon as possible for an evaluation.

You can also get in touch with a local support group for teens with Bipolar Disorder to join.

Knowing how to support your child during and after a mood change is important, as well as during their medical evaluation.

Bipolar in teens is a challenging condition to diagnose and manage, but understanding the condition and how to help a teen with the disorder is important.

# Here are some warning signs that a bipolar teen is using alcohol or drugs to self-medicate.

# Here are some warning signs that a bipolar teen is using alcohol or drugs to self-medicate.

## Introduction

Bipolar disorder is a serious mental illness. It can be difficult to detect because it often goes undiagnosed, even by professionals. Bipolar disorder is characterized by mood swings, rapid changes in energy and behavior, and intense euphoria or depression.

The vast majority of teens with bipolar disorder are also struggling with substance abuse issues.

These teenagers may also have other medical issues such as eating disorders or diabetes that impact their ability to stay sober while taking medicine for bipolar disorder.

Here's what you should look for if your child has been using alcohol or drugs to self-medicate:

## Using alcohol or drugs is a form of self-medication.

Self-medicating is a form of self-care. It's important for teens to know that there are many ways to treat mental health problems, including getting professional help from a doctor or therapist.

Self-medication can be dangerous if you don't know what you're doing and how much alcohol or drugs it will take to get the desired effect.

For example, some people use alcohol as a way to forget about their problems by drinking more alcohol than they usually would—and this can lead them into serious trouble if they have an accident while driving or falling asleep at night without remembering important things like where they are going next day or who lives in their house.

If someone self-medicates with something like marijuana (marijuana), for example, there is no such thing as "just one joint" because using this drug over time will cause dependence on it (a condition where continued use becomes necessary for survival

**Here are some warning signs that a bipolar teen is using alcohol or drugs to self-medicate.**

A person who uses marijuana regularly may need more than just one hit every now and then; he/she might even start craving certain types of food before going out somewhere with friends because he knows that taking those foods will make him feel better physically after drinking too much coffee earlier in the day!

**Teenagers who are depressed and have bipolar disorder try to self-medicate.**

Depression and bipolar disorder are two separate conditions.

They can coexist, but it's important to know that when someone has depression and also has a family history of bipolar disorder, they may be more likely to develop the condition.

Depression is a mood disorder that causes:

- Feelings of sadness,
- Worthlessness or hopelessness;
- Lethargy;
- Trouble sleeping;
- Decreased appetite or overeating;
- Low energy levels;
- Irritability or anger (especially if you're feeling down about yourself);
- Anhedonia (a loss of pleasure in life)

- Depression can be treated with medication such as lithium or bupropion hydrochloride, which helps regulate chemicals in your brain called neurotransmitters like serotonin, which affect how you feel emotionally as well as physically by increasing noradrenaline (the "fight or flight" hormone) while reducing serotonin levels.

- This often results in fatigue along with other symptoms such as headaches due to low blood pressure caused by dehydration.

**Here are some warning signs that a bipolar teen is using alcohol or drugs to self-medicate.**

Marijuana, alcohol, and diet pills are all common self-medications for teenagers.

- Drugs and alcohol are not effective at treating bipolar disorder.
- Marijuana is a depressant, which can make depression worse.
- Alcohol is a depressant and can make depression worse. It also has other effects on the body that may cause insomnia, anxiety, or irritability in people with bipolar disorder.
- The same goes for diet pills: they're all stimulants—
    - a category that includes caffeine as well as prescription drugs like Adderall® and Ritalin®.
    - Some studies have shown that these drugs make it harder for people with bipolar disorder to recover from episodes of mania or depression in some cases!

The following behaviors might indicate that your teen is using alcohol or drugs to self-medicate.

- ➢ Changes in sleeping habits: Your teen may experience a change in their sleep schedule. This could happen when they start using alcohol or drugs, but it could also be due to other reasons.
- ➢ Changes in eating habits: Your teen may be eating less than normal or more often than usual because they are using alcohol or drugs. You should talk to your child about having healthy meals and snacks, whether at home or school, so that you can make sure they get enough food each day without resorting to harmful substances like drugs or alcohol.
- ➢ Social life changes: If your teenager has recently started drinking heavily then this could mean that he/she is more likely to drop out of school completely (and possibly also take up smoking). It's important for parents who care about their children's future success at school not only want them succeed academically but also socially as well!
- ➢ Your teenager has become more rebellious or withdrawn for no apparent reason, you may want to talk to a mental health professional about the possibility that your teen may be depressed and/or manic.
- ➢ Your teenager may be depressed or manic.

**Here are some warning signs that a bipolar teen is using alcohol or drugs to self-medicate.**

If you notice that your teen has become more rebellious, withdrawn, and/or self-destructive for no apparent reason, you may want to talk to a mental health professional about the possibility that your teen might have bipolar disorder.

It's also possible that your teen has a sudden increase in energy followed by a sudden decrease in energy—sometimes referred to as hypomania or mania—that can last for several days before returning back toward normalcy (mania).

**Many teens with bipolar disorder also suffer from substance abuse.**

Many teens with bipolar disorder also suffer from substance abuse.

For example, a study of people age 18 or older found that those who had been diagnosed with bipolar disorder were twice as likely to have a substance abuse problem than other adults in the population.

This finding may be due to the fact that teens and young adults are more likely to use drugs or alcohol as self-medication for their symptoms.

The link between bipolar disorder and substance abuse can be seen in another way: Those who experience mania are at higher risk of developing an addiction than those who don't experience mania; this is why it's important for people with bipolar disorder—and their families—to get help early on before they become addicted!

**Asking questions and getting help as soon as possible will make it easier for you to help your teenager manage his bipolar disorder and stay sober at the same time.**

If you suspect your teen is using drugs or alcohol, talk to them about it.

Tell her that you know she's hurting herself and ask if she has any questions or concerns about what's going on in her life. Ask her how long she's been feeling depressed, irritable, anxious or angry lately and how often those feelings happen.

**Here are some warning signs that a bipolar teen is using alcohol or drugs to self-medicate.**

If the answers aren't clear cut—for example, if your child says he's been having trouble sleeping at night but nothing else seems out of the ordinary—it's important to get help as soon as possible.

A therapist can help guide your child through his mental health struggles while they're still young enough not only respond positively but also learn strategies for managing his disorder through therapy sessions scheduled on a regular basis (such as once per week).

There are many signs of drug or alcohol use in teens with bipolar disorder - Some very clear warning signs of alcohol or drugs use are:

1. Red eyes - Red eyes are a sign of dehydration. If you notice someone's eyes have turned red, they could be dehydrated. Dehydration causes blood vessels to dilate, causing the eyes to appear red.
2. Stiffness  - If someone seems stiff, they might be suffering from muscle cramps. Muscle cramps occur when muscles become tense and tight and cause them to contract. When this happens, the person feels pain and stiffness.
3. Headaches - Headaches are often caused by dehydration. Someone who is dehydrated will feel headaches. In addition, if someone has been drinking heavily, they may experience a hangover headache. Hangovers happen when someone drinks too much alcohol and then goes without food or water for several hours.
4. Dizziness - Dizziness is a symptom of dehydration. People who are dehydrated will often feel dizzy.
5. Nausea  - Nausea is a feeling of sickness or queasiness. Someone who is experiencing nausea might be nauseous due to dehydration.
6. Fatigue - Fatigue is a symptom of dehydration and malnutrition. A person who is tired might not eat enough or drink enough water.
7. Dry mouth  - A dry mouth is a symptom of dehydration, which means that a person does not have enough fluids in their body.

**Conclusion**

If your teen is using alcohol or drugs to self-medicate, it's important that you get help immediately. The sooner you can find out what's wrong and get treatment for the bipolar disorder, the better off both of you will be.

# Tracking Down Mental Health Experts

## Tracking Down Mental Health Experts

Finding a mental health professional can sometimes feel like the most difficult step in treating a mental health condition. An expert in mental health who you can trust and who knows their stuff will be a great help. Finding this ally or putting together a team of allies may require some patience and perseverance. Using the strategy below, you can find someone with whom you feel at ease working.

**Consider who you are looking for in Step 1**

People consult mental health professionals for a variety of reasons.
- Are you looking for a person with a prescription-writing license?
- Or are you primarily seeking a conversation partner?

A mental health condition is typically treated by at least two different professionals, one of whom focuses on medication (the biological side) and the other on emotional or behavioral therapies (the mind side).

**Here are some ideas to consider:**

You should visit a doctor for a physical examination if you haven't already spoken with one. Many conditions can manifest symptoms resembling those of mental illness. Tell a doctor about your symptoms even if you don't think your condition will need medical attention, and get a diagnosis.

A psychiatrist or other mental health professional, as opposed to your primary care physician, should be consulted if you have a mental health condition that could benefit from medication.

Although your primary care physician is a valuable partner in managing your overall health, a specialist has more experience handling conditions similar to yours.

Find a therapist or counselor if you need assistance with your emotions, behaviors, or thought patterns. You can find a therapist or counselor who is knowledgeable about your particular condition because they have specialties just like doctors do.

You can begin utilizing other forms of support if you have to wait for an appointment. There are free peer support groups available, such as those run by NAMI. You might also be able to get in touch with certified peer specialists in your state through your local mental health authority.

Do you think it would be beneficial to have a social worker on your treatment team if you needed help with your housing and employment, had multiple health issues, or had financial difficulties receiving care?

## Step 2: Gather referrals in

If you have health insurance, begin by dialing the information line for your provider. Request the phone numbers of local professionals who take your insurance. Just in case, try to get at least three names and phone numbers. Additionally, this is a good time to inquire about your insurance benefits.

The following are some possible queries:

Does a primary care physician need to be seen first in order to refer you to a psychiatrist, or can you schedule an appointment directly with them?

How does your plan handle paying for therapy sessions? Insurance plans can differ significantly in their treatment of therapy.

If you require treatment for a particular ailment, such as addiction or an eating disorder, request doctors who are experts in that area.

If you don't have health insurance, your local community mental health center should be your first port of call. You can look up the phone number at a public library or in a phone book.

## Step 3: Place the Call

If you find it difficult to make the call, ask a friend or member of your family to call on your behalf. Set up a meeting. Tell the person on the phone if this is your first time requesting a diagnosis so that they can schedule enough time for a productive conversation.

It would be prudent to schedule an appointment even if you are informed that new patients must wait several months for one. If you discover someone who can assist you right away, you can always reschedule your initial appointment.

Joining the waiting list for cancellations is another way to get an appointment sooner. You might be given an earlier appointment than you anticipated if a patient cancels at the last minute.

Visit your primary care physician as soon as you can to receive treatments and support to keep you going until you have your team put together if you feel you can't wait weeks or months for assistance. And if you find yourself in an emergency, kindly head straight to the emergency room of a hospital.

**Step 4: Make inquiries.**

When you first see a doctor or therapist, you "shop around" while also looking for advice. It makes sense to have inquiries. Be forthright when stating that you are looking for a long-term partner.

Here are some queries you may wish to consider or put forth:

- Do you feel at ease around this person?
    - The most crucial factor is whether you get along with this person, regardless of their reputation or level of education.
- How does it "feel" to you?
    - You might occasionally feel uncomfortable answering the personal questions a mental health professional asks, but the person shouldn't. You should have the impression that they are on your side.
- What level of education and work experience does this person possess?
- Has this person had experience with individuals like me? How much time?
- How will you collaborate to set objectives and monitor your progress?
- What can you anticipate if you collaborate?
    - How frequently will you meet, and how difficult will it be to schedule a meeting?
    - Can you email or call in between appointments?
    - What kinds of advancements can you anticipate?

Bring up your ability to pay insurance deductibles and co-pays as soon as possible if you're concerned.

Inquire about discounts or a sliding scale for payment. It's crucial to continue treatment without interruption, so doctors and therapists would like to be aware of any potential issues beforehand.

If finding a provider who respects and understands your cultural background is important to you, NAMI has some advice to help you do that.

**Step 5 : Build A Relationship**

The first person you see may occasionally not "feel right" or lack knowledge of your specific mental health condition.

Continue your search and call the next number on your list.

Keep in mind that you are building a team that will support your ongoing treatment. If you are persistent enough, you can find people who will listen to you, consider your viewpoint, and collaborate with you to enhance your sense of wellbeing.

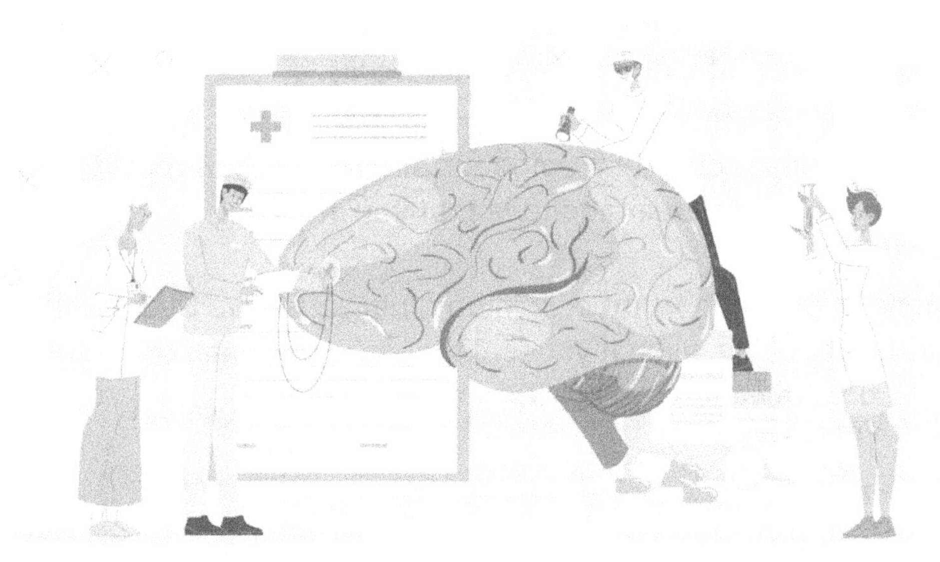

# Acknowledging Your Diagnoses

# Acknowledging Your Diagnoses

When a mental health condition is diagnosed, some people feel relief and hope. Some people might think that a diagnosis is "just words."

You might even experience conflicting emotions at once, such as relief that your problems now have names but fear and rage that you are ill.

Receiving a diagnosis is an important step in obtaining effective treatment and enhancing your quality of life, even if you feel that it carries unfavorable or damaging connotations and do not want to accept it.

## Acquiring a diagnosis

There is no medical test that can diagnose mental illness, unlike diabetes or cancer.

A physical examination and ongoing monitoring are two things a medical professional can do during an evaluation to rule out any underlying medical conditions that might be the source of symptoms.

A person may be referred to a mental health professional who will use The Diagnostic and Statistical Manual of Mental Disorders, Fifth Edition (DSM-5) to make a diagnosis after other medical conditions have been ruled out.

A person must meet a number of requirements, including feelings, symptoms, and behaviors over time, as listed in the DSM-5, which was published by the American Psychiatric Association.

## Why a Diagnosis Is Important

A medical professional will ask you about your history of symptoms in order to make a diagnosis.

A doctor may occasionally order a few medical tests to rule out potential physical illnesses, but we are unable to assess mental health on its own through blood tests or other biometric data.

Instead, medical professionals analyze your set of symptoms in light of what is known about mental health.

# Acknowledging Your Diagnoses

A diagnosis is a crucial tool that both you and your doctor can use. Your doctor or therapist will use the diagnosis to discuss your treatment options and potential health risks with you.

A diagnosis is important because it informs health insurance providers that you have a condition that necessitates medical attention.

Additionally, a medical diagnosis is required in order to be eligible for Social Security disability benefits or for Americans with Disabilities Act job protection.

Although naming your symptoms won't necessarily make them go away, congratulate yourself on making progress toward receiving treatment and defending your rights.

**Next Steps**

You might already be as knowledgeable as you can be when it comes to mental illness, or you might be learning about it for the first time.

A diagnosis is a good place to start when trying to find out more in either situation.

Take notes during your doctor's discussion of your condition so you can later look up the details of the diagnosis. Request books and websites with more information from your doctor.

When you read about your condition, you might find that some of your symptoms are similar to what you read about while others are not. That is typical.

Concentrate on understanding symptoms and remedies. It's possible to read depressing predictions about how serious mental illness cannot be "cured."

However, you can lessen or even get rid of your symptoms with treatment.

A diagnosis is not a death sentence; it is a starting point for effective treatment.

This is a good time to connect with other people who have your condition if you haven't already done so in a support group. Peer-to-Peer classes and discussion groups can offer support and suggestions from those who are coping successfully with their mental illnesses.

# Acknowledging Your Diagnoses

**What Happens If You Don't Agree With Your Diagnoses?**

You might have some queries for your doctor after reading about your condition.

- How do your symptoms more closely resemble this diagnosis than another?
- Can't it possibly be something else?
- What if it's a misunderstanding or a physical illness instead?

It's important to believe that your doctor explored every option. But don't immediately stop consulting with your doctor if you disagree with their assessment.

The diagnosis is merely a tool to aid you and your doctor in addressing your symptoms, which are already known to your doctor. If at all possible, stick with a doctor who is familiar with you. Not whether you agree with the diagnosis, but whether you can cooperate with this physician.

- Does your doctor listen to you when you express your worries?
- Try to respond to your inquiries?
- Does your doctor express remorse?
- Can i comprehend your objectives?
- What course of treatment does the doctor advise to help you achieve those objectives?

Think about whether you and the doctor can "agree to disagree" on the specifics of the diagnosis while still agreeing to follow the doctor's advice for a specified amount of time.

**Assessing a diagnosis**

A diagnosis' value depends on the course of treatment it recommends. It's crucial to periodically reevaluate your diagnosis, whether or not you feel confident in it.

You should meet with your doctor to discuss your progress after undergoing treatment for a while.

# Acknowledging Your Diagnoses

If treatment doesn't seem to be improving your condition, think about why.

If the current course of treatment is ineffective, you may want to consider other options or change your diagnosis.

A mental health professional determines the most accurate diagnosis they can given the available data.

He or she will observe you, pay attention to you, and gather fresh data as you work together over time to help hone your diagnosis.

The investigation into how to improve your life has started with your diagnosis.

# What Children Want to Know About When a Parent Has Bipolar Disorder

## What Children Want to Know About When a Parent Has Bipolar Disorder

When a member of the family is ill, children have many questions. When children don't get the answers they want to their questions, they often make up their own, which can be frightening and inaccurate!

When a family member has bipolar disorder, it frequently turns into a taboo subject that no one discusses.

To help them understand bipolar disorder, all kids need age-appropriate explanations and supports.

The "beginning conversation" about bipolar disorder between a parent and child will vary depending on the child's age and capacity for handling the information.

You are the expert on your kids.

Whether you are a healthy parent, a parent who has bipolar disorder, a grandparent, or another adult in the child's life, this guide will assist you in getting ready to take the first step.

This guide will provide you with additional information to help you continue the conversation with a child about bipolar disorder if you have already begun doing so.

It includes questions that kids frequently ask about their parents' bipolar disorder, as well as advice on how to respond to those questions.

**Children ask questions**

Bipolar disorder:
- What is it?
- What causes bipolar disorder?

Bipolar disorder is a condition that has an impact on a person's emotions, thoughts, and behavior. A brain disease is what it is.

When a person has bipolar disorder, their brain does not function normally.

We think, feel, and act in particular ways thanks to our brains..

Bipolar disorder causes people to think, feel, and act differently than they do when they are healthy.

Bipolar disorder typically has two distinct phases: lows known as depression and highs known as mania.

The individual is depressed and frequently withdraws during a low phase.

Depression is what this is.

The person is either excessively happy or excessively angry when they are in a high mood. The individual is more vivacious and outgoing than usual. Mania describes this.

The person is otherwise the same as they usually are.

Being bipolar is not a sign of weakness.

Depending on the individual, bipolar disorder may be mild or a more challenging struggle.

- Why does my father behave in this manner?
- How does having bipolar disorder feel?
- When my mother is not herself, what goes through her mind?

People with bipolar disorder behave differently from how they typically do.

It is bipolar disorder that is to blame for the mood swings. The emotional cycle.

One parent remarked, *"It was very hard because I felt I could do anything when I was high. I ate poorly, slept poorly, and overspent financially.*

The lows were extremely crippling; *I was unable to get out of bed, lost interest in everything, including myself, my work, my hobbies, and my friends.*

## What Children Want to Know About When a Parent Has Bipolar Disorder

The challenging part is the depression. It is challenging to get out of bed because of it.

- What does depression or "low mood" mean?
- How does it appear?

People who are in a bad mood might cry a lot and feel sad. Additionally, they might become more agitated and angry than usual.

- A depressed parent might not want to engage in activities such as playing, conversing, or taking the family on trips.
- They may easily become tired and spend a significant amount of time in bed.
- Sometimes their low moods make it difficult for them to focus or think clearly.
- They might worry a lot more than usual due to their depressed moods.
- Their reasoning might seem odd.
- They might not think highly of themselves or have a negative attitude toward life.

- What does mania, or a "high mood," mean?
- How does it appear?

When someone is in a good mood, they might feel like they are in control of everything, possess "super powers," and be able to accomplish anything.

One parent described it as:
- Constantly feeling extremely excited about something.
- They may also spend more money,
- Behave strangely,
- Or dress differently.
- High spirits, though, can also make them irritable and impatient.
- They might appear disengaged,
- Talk very quickly,
- Make snap judgments.
- They might have less of a desire to sleep.

## What Children Want to Know About When a Parent Has Bipolar Disorder

- What effects will bipolar disorder have on me?
- What impact will it have on my family?

Both the patient with the illness and other family members may be impacted by bipolar disorder in a variety of ways.

Because a parent with bipolar disorder may act or say things that make kids feel bad, scared, sad, angry, or frequently confused, it can be very difficult for kids to live with them.

This may occur if the parent is in a happy or unhappy mood. It may appear that a parent who experiences mood swings is more concerned with his or her own thoughts and feelings than with the opinions and feelings of the children at times.

People with bipolar disorder may not always want to talk about it because it can make them feel ashamed.

Do not forget that individuals with bipolar disorder will experience their typical moods in between high and low moods.

Slowly, the person starts acting more like himself or herself again as the high or low mood improves.

- What triggers bipolar illness?
- How does it get going?

Bipolar disorder is brought on by the brain's chemical balance being out of whack. However, we are unsure of the precise cause of the chemical imbalance. Sometimes symptoms can come on suddenly and for no apparent reason. In other instances, the symptoms appear to follow a crisis in life, stress, or an illness.

It's also possible for bipolar disorder to run in families. It won't typically be passed on to children, though. Bipolar disorder affects about one in ten children whose parents have the illness.

It is unknown why some people are more susceptible to developing bipolar disorder than others.  The bipolar disorder of the parent is not brought on by the child.

# Long-term Consequences for Children Of Having A Mother Who Suffers from Bipolar Disorder.

## Long-term consequences for children of having a mother who suffers from bipolar disorder.

After giving birth, mothers with bipolar disorder are more likely to experience a relapse.

The consequences of bipolar parenting can leave long-lasting scars.

Early intervention may be the best practice for avoiding the consequences of being raised by a bipolar mother.

This condition not only disrupts and challenges the living environment, but it can also raise concerns about the disorder developing in the future.

Naturally, there is concern that the bipolar mother's genes will be passed down to future generations.

On the other hand, learning how to manage symptoms of bipolar disorder such as anxiety and depression can be accomplished throurk.

### Recognizing Bipolar Disorder

- Bipolar disorder is a mental health disorder that can last a lifetime and interfere with daily life.
- Bipolar disorder can cause mood and energy swings. Despite the fact that bipolar disorder is a long-term condition, there are many ways to treat and find relief from it.
- Bipolar disorder alters how the brain reacts and feels in certain situations. This mental condition can experience two distinct phases of lows and highs. The low periods are associated with depression symptoms, whereas the high periods are known as mania.

### The Low Phase

The low phase is characterized by feelings of extreme depression and sadness.

Withdrawal from friends and family is common during this period of lows. During this time, the person with bipolar disorder may withdraw and isolate themselves from family and friends.

## Long-term consequences for children of having a mother who suffers from bipolar disorder.

Irritation and illogical sadness are frequently associated with bipolar disorder.

Furthermore, symptoms of being overly tired may occur, resulting in more time spent in bed than previously done. Crying in solitude has been linked to the low phase of bipolar disorder.

**Maximum Phase**

In contrast to the low phase's depression and sadness, the high phase of mania includes different emotions, such as being overly happy and more outgoing.

Mania-related stage represent a change in normal behavior that is visible to friends and family.

Mania symptoms can begin to interfere with daily life, including work, school, and relationships.

During this stage of bipolar disorder, people may dress differently, spend more money, and speak faster. Bipolar's two phases can be diametrically opposed and cycle in a circle every month or week.

These shifting moods and emotions can have an impact on children as a result of bipolar parenting.

Although children cannot magically cure this mental illness, there are things a family can do to assist.

**Future Prospects**

Despite the fact that there is no direct cure for bipolar disorder, there are several treatments for bipolar parenting available so that mothers can get the help they need when raising children.

Getting treatment is one of the best ways to cope with bipolar and be a parent. Talk therapy and group therapy can be used to provide coping mechanisms for people suffering from bipolar disorder.

**Long-term consequences for children of having a mother who suffers from bipolar disorder.**

Medication, in addition to therapy, can be used to alleviate the symptoms of bipolar disorder.

Mood stabilizers, antipsychotics, and antidepressants are some of the medications used to treat this disorder. Prescription medications can be based on the specific symptoms expressed.

Mood stabilizers can help regulate symptoms of a manic episode, while antidepressants can help regulate symptoms of a depressive episode.

If mood stabilizers and antidepressants do not alleviate symptoms of depression and mania, antipsychotic medications may be used.

These medications can help with overall mood and can be prescribed alone or in conjunction with a mood stabilizer.

## Being Raised by a Bipolar Mother

Because bipolar disorders are frequently misdiagnosed or completely ignored, many children grow up with a mother who has erratic moods and behaviors and have no idea why.

Mental illnesses such as bipolar disorder can cause children to assume parental responsibilities.

A lack of safety and care from a bipolar parent can cause worry and difficulty making decisions.

Bipolar disorders can cause traumatic childhoods and even mental health problems in children raised by bipolar mothers later in life.

Children raised by untreated bipolar mothers can suffer long-term consequences.

## Problems with Trust

According to research, turbulent childhoods lead to trust issues, and a bipolar mother faces the same risk.

# Long-term consequences for children of having a mother who suffers from bipolar disorder.

Bipolar disorder can cause chaos and unreliability, leaving the child fearful.

It can be difficult to open up and trust new people as an adult without the constant stability of a parent. Feelings of distrust can make it difficult to find a partner, commit to a job, and achieve good grades.

## Characteristics of Self-blame

Young children may have difficulty understanding mental illness and may blame themselves for their parent's disorder.

Feelings of guilt may arise instead of rationalizing the bipolar mother's behavior as a result of mental illness.

Feelings of self-blame may arise as a result of thoughts about how the child's actions may be causing the parent's bipolar disorder to have depression or mania.

Unfortunately, feelings of guilt and responsibility for anything that goes wrong can persist into adulthood.

For children of bipolar parents, carrying the burden of self-blame can be devastating.

## Obsessive-Compulsive Disorder (OCD) (OCD)

Obsessive-compulsive disorder is another common long-term effect of growing up in a household with a bipolar parent (OCD). Children who lack structure and routine may seek control in stressful situations.

Children of bipolar mothers may follow the rules in the hope that their mother will improve and become more stable.

Control is a coping mechanism that can develop in childhood but can lead to problems in adulthood.

OCD is commonly associated with distressing thoughts and behaviors that interfere with daily life.

**Long-term consequences for children of having a mother who suffers from bipolar disorder.**

OCD symptoms frequently include:

- Persistent fear of dirt and pathogens
- Fear of not knowing
- The need to arrange and categorize everything
- Persistent and unwanted thoughts
- Depression and anxiety

Children whose mothers have bipolar disorder have two of the most terrible long-term effects are depression and anxiety.

Bipolar disorder is unpredictable, which can cause others to feel depressed or anxious.

Mothers with bipolar disorder may frequently exhibit maternal neglect, which increases the risk that high-risk children will develop anxiety and mood disorders like depression.

If the child stays in touch with their bipolar mother as they get older, it can sometimes feel impossible to deal with these emotions.

The best way to reduce a child's risk of developing anxiety and mood disorders is through early intervention.

**Self-care is of utmost importance.**

The child of a mother who suffers from bipolar disorder might find it challenging to accept that their actions cannot cure or improve their mother.

Children who have parents who suffer from bipolar disorder may feel pressured to treat their parents' symptoms. If support and assistance are not received, these pressures may persist into adulthood.

Children of mothers with bipolar disorder may place the highest priority on their mental health. The child's mental health can be given priority in order to support the mother through the various bipolar phases.

## Long-term consequences for children of having a mother who suffers from bipolar disorder.

Neglecting joy and serenity can make it difficult to support the bipolar mother's support system. Without controlling the symptoms brought on by the mother's bipolar disorder, goals can be difficult to achieve.

**A community to join.**

The difficulties that come with having a bipolar mother during childhood can make it seem like the mother is the only one who suffers from the condition.

However, growing up and entering adulthood can make it simpler to understand the disorder and make it possible to get more support from people who share that understanding.

In terms of managing unexpected stress and juggling family and work life, finding a community of people with bipolar mothers can be life-changing.

Even though some support groups meet in person, it is possible to find online resources to connect with others who share an understanding of bipolar disorder.

Online communities are a great way to meet people who share your upbringing and are readily available.

Feelings of isolation brought on by family issues and bipolar disorder can be alleviated by seeking solace from others who understand them. A necessary break from the strain of having a bipolar mother can be found in support groups.

**Take Up Walking**

As important as it is to be there for those who have bipolar disorder, learning to walk away is another crucial piece of bipolar disorder advice.

Depending on the day and which phase the bipolar is in, bipolar disorders can be distinguished by either a low or high mood. Setting limits can be essential for improving mental health.

**Long-term consequences for children of having a mother who suffers from bipolar disorder.**

Regular child care for the bipolar mother is not in the child's best interests.

Putting off life can be harmful to the child and the mother, who has bipolar disorder.

Having bipolar disorder can lead to mood swings from day to day, *so knowing when to leave a situation is a crucial skill.*

**Accept Your Narrative**

Numerous books and films have been produced about kids whose mother suffers from bipolar disorder. But no matter how many books or movies are read or watched, it can be challenging to accept your childhood after having a mother with bipolar disorder.

It might be necessary to do some inner work in order to progress and find peace.

Accepting one's childhood, experiences in life, and mother's bipolar disorder can improve one's adult life.

It can take time to recover from adverse childhood and life experiences because the process is not linear. A great place to start is by contacting a mental health professional.

**Receive therapy.**

Treatment can be a helpful tool, regardless of whether the challenges of having a mother with bipolar disorder have led to symptoms of mental illness or the mother's characteristics have been passed on to the child.

Understanding a mental health treatment can help you avoid severe anxiety, depression, OCD, and other distressing symptoms.

Treatment facilities can offer a place where people can discuss mental health struggles without feeling judged.

**Long-term consequences for children of having a mother who suffers from bipolar disorder.**

Although a parent cannot be replaced, children of bipolar parents can benefit from finding places of solace, joy, and support.

As a therapist, talking to people who aren't directly involved in the situation might be beneficial.

The difficulties and frustration with the bipolar parent can now be expressed freely without restraint or concern for the parent's finding out.

Growing up with a bipolar mother presents a number of challenges during infancy as well as into adulthood. There is, however, always hope for living a normal life. In order to manage the consequences of having grown up with a bipolar mother.

**Fighting the Bipolar Stigma and Succeeding as an Adult**

It is crucial to fight the stigma associated with bipolar disorder and other mental health issues.

Disorders of the mind are medical conditions that are subject to scrutiny and judgment from others. Understanding the causes, symptoms, and medical nature of bipolar disorder can help lessen the stigma associated with it.

Children of bipolar parents are more likely to experience anxiety, depression, and OCD symptoms as a coping mechanism. However, receiving treatment for these issues will enable these kids to thrive as adults.

# A Day in the Life of a Bipolar Disorder & Personal Narratives

A Day in the Life of a bipolar disorder is a heartfelt and honest day-by-day look at living with bipolar disorder, from the patients perspective.

It's a full-blown struggle in your every day life. But you're stronger than you know.

You will overcome this obstacle and meet your true potential.

BP disorder can be exhausting, frustrating and overwhelming. But it doesn't have to be.

Through this story and the stories of others, I hope to help provide a greater understanding of this disease by sharing stories that range from the lighthearted to the dark and disturbing.

But most importantly,

I hope these stories will inspire you to reach out for help or take another step in searching for a solution..

## My Daily Plight with Bipolar by Elissa Harrington

If you have bipolar disorder and are reading this guide, you may be someone who struggles with managing their emotions.

In this section, I'll talk about my own experiences with bipolar disorder with a central focus on the daily challenges that come with this illness and intimate details of life on the cusp of change.

It's tough to admit you have a mental illness and it's even tougher to talk about it with other people.

It's really hard to grapple with this disorder alone, which is why writing can help us deal with it. Anyone who has been diagnosed with bipolar disorder will tell you about their experience of being out of control and having zebra-like recovery periods.

It can be as terrifying and overwhelming as it is exciting and exhilarating. I believe it's time for more people to know who I am and what I've been through.

My darkest days have taught me how to turn my life around, but I've never felt more alone than when I'm in the midst of a manic episode.

There are times when I feel lost and cannot stand myself because of the amount of energy I'm using to manage my illness. In fact, I find that I have not enough energy to do what is expected from me;

I'm sitting here in my room, looking around. I don't know what to do with myself. There is so much going on in my head right now, but nothing I can do about it. It's 11:00 p.m. and I can't sleep.

I've been lying in bed for hours, thoughts racing through my mind. I'm exhausted, but my mind won't shut off. I try to relax, but it's impossible. I'm restless, irritable, and on the verge of tears. I know I need to get some shut-eye, but I can't.

It seems like every second of every day there is something else to worry about or something else that needs done. My mind is racing faster than a bullet train through the desert and I can feel the panic rising up inside me like water from a well.

My heart is pounding and my mouth feels dryer than the Sahara Desert in July. My hands are shaking and my palms are drenched in sweat. I can feel my body tensing up, just like it does when I'm about to have a panic attack.

**69**

### My Daily Plight with Bipolar by Elissa Harrington

My heart is racing faster than a bullet train through the desert and I can feel the panic rising up inside me like water from a well.

My mind is racing faster than a bullet train through the desert and I can feel the panic rising up inside me like water from a well.

This is a typical night for me, and I never know when the next dip is going to hit.

I've been dealing with bipolar disorder for years, and I've learned to manage it with medication and therapy.

It's something that I'll never be cured of, but I've learned to manage it.

I take medication, see a therapist, and have a support system of family and friends.

I've also found that writing is a helpful way to cope with my bipolar disorder. Through writing, I can explore my thoughts and feelings, and make sense of my chaotic mind.

Writing is a form of self-care for me, and it's something that I truly enjoy. It's a way for me to connect with others who have similar experiences, and it helps me to feel less alone.

But there are still times when it feels like it's running my life. Times when I can't sleep, can't focus, can't eat, can't work, can't function. Times when I'm so petrified of the next low that I can't enjoy the high. It's hard to explain what it's like to live with bipolar disorder.

It's hard to explain the fear, the exhaustion, the frustration, the hopelessness. But I'm not going to give up. I'm going to keep fighting, because I know there's hope for a better tomorrow.

Mental illness doesn't have to consume someone's life to be prevalent. In many cases, it's simply a daily battle that requires extra effort, understanding, and strength. For me, writing is one way that I'm able to keep fighting.

Some days are good. I'm productive, happy, and full of energy. But other days are bad. I'm depressed, anxious, and completely drained. On those days, it's all I can do to get out of bed and get dressed.

## My Daily Plight with Bipolar by Elissa Harrington

Mental illness is often misunderstood and stigmatized. But the reality is that mental illness is very real and can be very debilitating.

Bipolar disorder is one type of mental illness that can be particularly tricky to manage.

There are many different types of bipolar disorder and treatment can bring many kinds of help-emotional, physical and spiritual for example. It all depends upon you! Your attitude will make all the difference in how you feel about the situation, and what works best for you.

I think it's important to remember that even in the worst of times, there is hope.

Sometimes I can't sleep, can't concentrate or focus, can't eat or function; which means that sometimes I want to give up on everything and myself.

Then there are other times where I don't feel like giving up at all because for every moment of darkness there's a moment of light—it could be any time spent with family or friends or just being out in nature. You never know what tomorrow will bring.

There are many things that help me when I'm feeling like I can't get out of bed or when my panic attacks feel overwhelming.

Sometimes it's music, sometimes it's exercise and yoga, sometimes its taking a long walk in the sunshine.

Sometimes it's doing something to help others (like volunteering at an animal shelter) or helping yourself (like going to the gym).

There are a lot of ways to deal with bipolar disorder—and I'm determined to figure out the best one for me!

Remember to take care of yourself now, because when an episode comes along; it will just be harder to deal with than before.

You need to keep your mind focused on your goals - setbacks are tough but they don't have to be fatal!

# Narrative 1 - My Wife is Bipolar: A Look at Her Life, How She's Feeling, and What We're Doing to Help Her.
## by Richard Dean

## Narrative 1 - My Wife is Bipolar: A Look at Her Life, How She's Feeling, and What We're Doing to Help Her by Richard Dean

After years of struggling with her mental health, my wife recently received the diagnosis of bipolar disorder II with schizoaffective disorder as well as PTSD, anxiety, and depression.

After I read through what was happening to her, and how common it was, I was surprised to find out that most people have no idea what these illnesses are or how to best support the person suffering from them. That's why I'm writing this article about my wife's condition.

**Going Backwards in Time**

From growing up in the 60's to having bipolar disorder today, my experiences with mental illness have been greatly impacted by social and economic factors. Growing up in a lower-income family, my mother struggled with bipolar disorder for much of her adult life. Because of this, we've learned a great deal about how people with mental health conditions are penalized and misunderstood.

- But what about our own lives?
- How do we respond when the stressors in our own lives are mental or emotional?
- What kind of impact do our thoughts have on our actions?

I'm writing from the perspective of a husband who has lived through my wife's manic episodes, depressive periods, anxiety attacks, mood swings and other symptoms.

I want to show readers how mental illness impacts not only the sufferer but also their friends and family members.

It can be very difficult to explain everything to someone who doesn't experience it themselves. I hope that I can provide some insight into living with someone who struggles with bipolar disorder without being too clinical or hard to understand.

Living with someone who suffers from depression is different than living with someone who suffers from manic depression. One partner may need medication while the other does not.

**Narrative 1 - My Wife is Bipolar: A Look at Her Life, How She's Feeling, and What We're Doing to Help Her by Richard Dean**

One person may be diagnosed as borderline personality disorder while another person has post traumatic stress disorder.

If you haven't experienced it yourself, you might never know the difference!

My wife's behavior varies depending on which type of mood she's in. Sometimes she'll get really anxious or manic, then she'll just seem like herself again (or as close to normal as possible).

Once I found out what was going on and got the proper diagnosis from a doctor, things became clearer. Now when one of these episodes happen we try to identify the trigger (if there is one) so that we can work together to find solutions. Usually the anxiety eases after a few days, but sometimes it lasts weeks before fading away.

And since anxiety and depression often go hand in hand, there are times when she will go back and forth between them over the course of several weeks or months. Other times they seem to hit all at once, making it impossible to figure out which one is causing the most trouble.

The best thing we can do during those tough moments is lean on each other and talk about what's going on. That way we don't feel isolated or alone with whatever feelings come up.

Our goal isn't necessarily always cure but rather treatment. With bipolar disorder, treatment involves finding ways to help manage your symptoms so that they don't interfere with your daily life. This includes medication, therapy, and support groups. Learning to live with bipolar disorder is a process.

There's no magic bullet or quick fix. There's no such thing as perfection. But the more knowledge we gain, the better we can help ourselves and others who struggle with mental illness of any kind. This guide is dedicated to exploring the ups and downs of living with bipolar disorder in hopes of giving others the tools needed to make informed decisions about their own future.

Whether you have bipolar disorder or not, the information here can help anyone who is dealing with a friend or family member who suffers from mental illness.

**Narrative 1 - My Wife is Bipolar: A Look at Her Life, How She's Feeling, and What We're Doing to Help Her by Richard Dean**

My wife's bipolar disorder is what brought us together and it's part of what keeps us strong.

**Now - Current Day**

Day to day life with my wife has been very tough lately,  in the last few months it seems like she has had a harder time coping with her symptoms.

It started with her sleeping less and talking more. When I got home from work, she would talk endlessly about everything that happened throughout the day. It became difficult for me to have a conversation because it felt like she didn't really want to listen or hear what I had to say.

I asked her if anything was wrong and she told me no but then said something out of left field that made no sense. Things just kept getting worse as time went on.. Her drinking is coming up often again as an excuse when we fight or disagree on something.

If I point this out to her, she'll get defensive and tell me I'm being too sensitive. She's become quick tempered when little things don't go as planned which leaves us feeling anxious all the time.

Last week she even left in the middle of dinner without telling anyone where she was going. All these changes are starting to take their toll on our marriage-especially since we can't seem to find any solutions for how to help her get better.

It's so hard to see her this way and not be able to do anything about it. The other night I came home from work early because she had gone into one of her manias, which ended up turning into a panic attack after hours of running around frantically trying to catch up on housework.

After finally calming down and lying down in bed together, she apologized saying that I know you're doing your best. With tears in her eyes, she explained that this mania had taken control of her mind and she couldn't think straight. That night she talked to me calmly and peacefully as though nothing ever happened. I held onto her tight until we both fell asleep next to each other.

She's been so much better ever since then! I never knew that mania could lead to manic hypersexuality - it must have been triggered by anxiety and overstimulation. It sounds like she didn't know either- now she knows, we know, and now we can steer clear of these triggers.

These past few days have been really great because every morning I've woken up to her smiling at me while watching tv (the calm before the storm). She used to sleep less than three hours a night during manias but now she's sleeping through the night every night which helps her stay well rested (we're still waiting for those miracle pills).

Her mood swings are always fast paced so it's hard for me keep up sometimes but overall I feel good knowing that she feels good (though the good days will eventually stop) and that she's looking forward to the future.

I worry about the mania, depression trigger and the future, but I'm thankful for the positive moments we're having. Sometimes it takes a lot of patience to handle bipolar disorder, but in the end it's worth it.

There's a huge difference between depression and mania. I had a brief period of depression once, but it wasn't as bad as this bipolar disorder that I experience on a daily basis.

Every day is different for me because the disease has to run its course which means highs and lows; however, we have good days and bad days but at least we're in this together, so we know that there's no need to live in fear. It's been a few weeks since she's had a mania and she is on medication so it's less likely to happen.  It's only when she gets really stressed out and then it starts to happen.

**Alcoholism**

This time it was because of the mania that I found out about her alcoholism which is a drug addiction that she's been hiding from me for years. It turns out she drinks almost everyday to relieve the stress and pressure.

I had no idea. She didn't drink at all when we first met, but now it's like she needs a drink to survive the day (or maybe two). Alcoholism is really sad because my wife doesn't drink to have fun or get drunk, but to make herself feel good (which only ends up making her feel worse).

**Narrative 1 - My Wife is Bipolar: A Look at Her Life, How She's Feeling, and What We're Doing to Help Her by Richard Dean**

She tries so hard for me and for our daughter that this news breaks my heart. I love her so much, and I know that she's a good person deep down. She wants to get better so badly but it's been hard for her because of the guilt and shame that she feels when drinking alcohol.

Her drug addiction stems from the low self-esteem and the anger that she feels about herself. My wife is a true fighter but we have to face this issue head on if we want to fix it. I feel like she hates me because of this news, but I can't blame her for being mad at me. It's been difficult for her as well which has caused her to lash out and say things in anger which really hurts me.

The addict and the alcoholic is a crazy combination and I don't know how to deal with it. One minute she's happy, and the next she's angry for seemingly no reason. Even though she hasn't shown any signs of mania in awhile, I don't want to risk it so we're going to start seeing a therapist who specializes in dual diagnosis patients because they're just that common nowadays.

To be honest, I am more scared of her going into a major depressive episode again then I am of another manic episode. Maybe that says something about me but at this point we'll take what we can get so as long as she's taking her meds and not abusing substances, we'll be okay.

**Next Steps**
It's been an emotional rollercoaster of mixed feelings. I'm feeling hopeful that this might be the beginning of something great for us.

One thing my wife has started is a group therapy session she goes to once a week. It's not always easy, but she tells me that they all have one thing in common - they want to learn how to better cope with their lives and live them more fully.

And as far as her family life is concerned, we've agreed on some rules and regulations that will help keep everyone happy.

My wife's father even offered to come over every Sunday night so we can go out together as a family.

The main takeaway from all of this? Don't give up hope. Living with a person suffering from bipolar disorder isn't easy, but you don't need to suffer alone.

**Narrative 1 - My Wife is Bipolar: A Look at Her Life, How She's Feeling, and What We're Doing to Help Her by Richard Dean**

Find a doctor you trust, take care of yourself and find ways to spend time together. If you both feel hopeless, reach out to a therapist or psychiatrist.

Above all else, never stop fighting for your loved one. They are worth fighting for.

In any case, if you're dealing with mental illness in your own life right now (or suspect that a friend or family member might be), don't hesitate to ask for professional advice and assistance.

After all, facing challenges head-on will make you stronger—and bring new perspective into your life too.

The next part of recovery is learning to manage stress.

Easier said than done, right?  However, there are steps you can take to lessen your stress.

Give yourself time to work on a daily basis—especially when it comes to taking care of children. You'll need the extra energy later on when everything feels like its spiraling out of control again.

Exercise is also important because it releases endorphins which provide an instant mood boost.

When things get tough, try these steps: talk about what's bothering you, plan how you'll deal with each problem, visualize solutions and think about people in your life who support you.

Share those worries when possible so others understand what's going on inside your head. This doesn't mean you should burden others with information they don't need to know, but talking helps release pent-up emotions.

For example, when my wife first shared her diagnosis with our daughter, the young girl cried and told her mommy that she had missed something so obvious-- something no one knew about but her!

Sometimes just listening is enough to lift spirits; children are often very observant.

Finally, when caring for children during a depressive episode, remember that it's not about doing everything right. Instead of expecting perfection from ourselves and our spouses/partners, we focus on improving small things here and there instead.

At first glance people may assume that living with someone struggling from bipolar disorder means giving up your own identity--but nothing could be further from the truth!

 Just as my wife's bipolar disorder doesn't define her, being a parent and raising children are equally important in shaping who we are.

The best thing we can do for our kids is to be open about the problems we're dealing with. Being honest about mental health issues not only encourages acceptance from the family, but it gives children the opportunity to develop empathy for those around them.

Most importantly, it teaches them that life is unpredictable and that sometimes things happen without warning or reason.

Teaching children how to handle stress will not only prepare them for adulthood, but it will show them that life is about solving problems together--even when you don't know how.

I love my wife with all of my heart, and there's nothing I wouldn't do for her in this world.

# Narrative 2 - What to Do When Your Child Is Diagnosed With Bipolar Disorder.
## by Letisha Crone

**Narrative 2 - What to Do When Your Child Is Diagnosed With Bipolar Disorder – by Letisha Crone**

When my daughter was diagnosed with bipolar disorder, I wasn't sure what to do next. She's the youngest in our family, and she's just 16 years old. As much as I wanted to get the best possible care for her, finding a reputable psychologist who specialized in bipolar disorder turned out to be much more difficult than I thought it would be. This article will help you find the answers you need and get your daughter on the road to recovery from bipolar disorder as quickly as possible.

**Stigma**

Sadly, there is still a great deal of stigma associated with mental illness. This can make it difficult for people to seek help or even talk about their experiences. When it comes to bipolar disorder, this stigma can be even more pronounced.

As the parent of a child with bipolar disorder, you may feel alone and unsure of what to do next. But there are resources and support available.

Here are some steps you can take when raising your child with bipolar disorder:
- - Get educated about the symptoms and treatments so that you know how to spot warning signs.
- - Be proactive in seeking treatment by contacting your doctor or mental health professional when warning signs arise.
- - Educate yourself on how to deal with stigma in order to empower your children who also have bipolar disorder. You will want them to learn how to advocate for themselves as well.
- - Seek out peer groups and family counseling in order to get support from others who understand the struggles of having a loved one with bipolar disorder. Talk therapy helps promote healthy coping skills while dealing with stigma.
- - Remember that many famous celebrities suffer from bipolar disorder, such as Lady Gaga, Demi Lovato, Jared Leto, and Brooke Shields. If they've been able to survive, then your child can too.
- - Continue talking to your kids about suicide and answer any questions they may have honestly. You'll want them to feel comfortable asking you anything at all. And when it comes to suicide, always let them know that suicide is not an option. We need to stop suicide stigma so people won't feel like they're being judged if they ask for help. It's a stigma that needs to go away.
- - Many parents struggle with stress after their child has been diagnosed with bipolar disorder. You may be wondering how your life will change and whether you can handle it all. It's important to remember that as parents, we're going through something new together, which makes us stronger than ever before.

## Narrative 2 - What to Do When Your Child Is Diagnosed With Bipolar Disorder – by Letisha Crone

- Having suicidal thoughts is common among those living with bipolar disorder. Suicide prevention efforts should include families and friends because these close relationships are critical for reducing suicide risk. Families and friends play an important role in helping identify suicide warning signs, providing emotional support, maintaining safety, and staying connected.

Mental illness isn't easy but there are ways to live through it and keep fighting every day until things start getting better.

**Recovery starts with selfcare, selflove, and mindfulness.**

- Selfcare is taking care of ourselves first instead of taking care of everyone else first.

- Selflove is treating ourselves the way we would treat someone else; give kindness to ourselves.

- Mindfulness is just focusing on our breath, thinking good thoughts instead of bad ones and refocusing our attention back onto breathing every time it wanders off onto dark paths.

**How does my daughter deal with the anxiety and stress of day to day living, with bipolar?**

1. First and foremost, it's important that she have a strong support system in place. This could include close friends or family members, a therapist, or a support group for people with bipolar disorder.

2. Secondly, it's important to practice self-care and self-love. This entails looking after her physical, emotional, and mental health. This could include things like exercise, eating a balanced diet, getting enough sleep, and spending time doing things she enjoys.

3. Thirdly, it's important to be mindful of her triggers and stressors. Identifying what sets off her bipolar episodes can help her avoid them or at least be prepared for them. For example, if she knows that being around alcohol will trigger an episode, then it would be good for her to avoid situations where alcohol is present. If she knows that making eye contact with strangers will trigger an episode, then avoiding strangers would be a good idea.

4.   Additionally, it's important to talk about suicide prevention as well as mental health awareness. It can be helpful to tell someone who is considering suicide about the resources available to them such as crisis hotlines and emergency rooms.

5.   We need to recognize that these illnesses are chronic conditions, not something that a person can just snap out of on their own. Acknowledge when they are going through mania, psychosis, depression, anxiety attacks, etc., so they know you understand what they're going through.

What to do when my daught is so depressed, that she cries all day and locks her self in her bedroom?

The first thing you need to do is find some way for your daughter to engage in self-care.

Even if she doesn't want to go outside, make sure she has plenty of activities inside her bedroom that are healthy for her such as reading a book, listening to music, drawing, or journaling.

You should also encourage her to practice mindfulness on a daily basis and get enough sleep every night.

If she does not feel safe going outside on her own due to fear of manic episodes, arrange for someone else (a friend or relative) take her on walks with them during which they may enjoy music together or listen attentively while talking about each other's thoughts and feelings in an attempt at normalizing their experiences with one another.

It can be so hard to see your child suffer from these debilitating mental illnesses, but it will be helpful for both of you if you keep reminding yourself that recovery is possible.

It can take years but it is possible! In the meantime, give yourself love by practicing self-care like eating right and exercising regularly.

And remember: the most important thing anyone can do when struggling with any type of mental illness is seek professional help early on! There are many different types of treatment options available--don't hesitate to ask questions until you're satisfied with the answers.

It can be difficult to know what to do when your child is diagnosed with bipolar disorder.

The first thing you should do is listen to your child's doctor and follow their recommendations.

It's important to keep in mind that bipolar disorder is a serious mental illness that can be effectively treated with medication and therapy. However, it's also important to understand that addiction, manic episodes, depression, and anxiety are all potential complications of the disorder.

If you're concerned about your child's well-being, don't hesitate to reach out to a mental health professional for help. You'll need to work together to create an individualized treatment plan based on your child's needs.

You might want to consider looking into services that offer counseling sessions, psychiatry appointments, or support groups tailored towards children who have bipolar disorder.

One common misconception about people who have bipolar disorder is that they can't control themselves and act out aggressively. In reality, it may be more challenging for people with this type of mental illness to restrain themselves from exhibiting erratic behavior during manic or depressive periods because there may not be as much activity in their prefrontal cortex as there would otherwise be if they were healthy .

People with bipolar disorder may experience depression, anxiety, ADHD, OCD, addiction, and borderline personality disorder alongside the other symptoms of bipolar I.  They may also develop co-occurring conditions like PTSD, substance abuse, chronic pain, schizophrenia, or psychosis.

These secondary conditions make recovery even more difficult for people living with bipolar disorder because they must manage two sets of symptoms simultaneously. For example: someone with both bipolar I and chronic pain will have to manage severe mood swings as well as managing chronic pain every day. For some people recovering from these conditions, it may be helpful to pursue alternative therapies like yoga or meditation in order to relieve stress and lower their level of arousal.

Others might find relief through psychotherapy; however talk therapy isn't always effective for everyone.

No parent wants to hear that their child has a mental illness, but it's important to remember that there are solutions. While it may be difficult, you can get through this with the help of professionals and support groups. Here are some things to keep in mind:

1. Don't blame yourself. It's easy to feel guilty when your child is diagnosed with a mental illness, but it's important to remember that you're not responsible. Mental illness is complex and often has multiple causes.

2. Seek professional help. A mental health professional can provide you with information and resources to help you understand and cope with your child's diagnosis.

3. Join a support group. There are many groups available for parents of children with mental illness. One such group is NAMI (National Alliance on Mental Illness). These organizations will connect you with other families who have been dealing with similar issues as well as provide you with practical advice.

As a parent, it's so hard to know what to do next when your child is diagnosed with bipolar disorder.

- What should I do?

- Should I just accept that my daughter will never recover?

- Am I being too harsh on her?

- Should I send her away or allow her to live at home while she goes through treatment?

All these questions are answered by professionals in NAMI. You need to focus on taking care of yourself and ensuring your child receives the best possible care. The first step would be to take her to a therapist because they can evaluate if she needs more specialized care from a psychiatrist or psychologist. She needs drug addiction recovery, selfcare, selflove, stigma relief, stress management and suicide prevention. Remember that mental illness does not discriminate against age- all races, genders and lifestyles are susceptible.

Mindfulness practices like meditation are helpful for helping reduce anxiety levels which could also lead someone into an episode of mania where he could start behaving impulsively again. If he does show signs of manic behavior then medication might be necessary-again medication doesn't mean we give up hope!

## Narrative 2 - What to Do When Your Child Is Diagnosed With Bipolar Disorder – by Letisha Crone

**Focus on Strengths**

It can be difficult to accept that your child has bipolar disorder, but it is important to remember that this is just one part of who they are.

There are many things that make up your child's identity and this should not define them. It is also important to remember that bipolar disorder is a treatable illness. Recovery is possible and there are many resources available to help you and your family.

You are not alone in this journey. It is okay to get emotional. It's okay if you don't always feel great.

Find people in your life who care about you and support you during this time- often people find themselves more connected with friends than they ever have been before because of these common experiences.

Talk with other parents going through the same thing, or find someone else struggling with mental health as well and share what helps work for you!

**The Importance of Resilience**

No parent wants to hear that their child has a mental illness. It's natural to feel scared, sad, and helpless when you receive this news. But it's important to remember that your child is still the same person they were before the diagnosis.

The more you can do to help them, the better off they'll be in the long run. Mental illnesses are not just about getting better; they are also about living well. Helping them recover can include taking care of yourself too so that you have enough energy for both of you.

 There are many online resources available to help with understanding different mental illnesses and connecting with other parents who share your experiences. If you don't know where to start, look at organizations like NAMI (National Alliance on Mental Illness) or AFSP (American Foundation for Suicide Prevention). You'll find information on bipolar disorder from people who understand what you're going through. For example, there are videos that give tips on how to cope with symptoms and provide insights into how others manage theirs. These people are in recovery themselves which means they know what it takes! After reading these articles I realized that my daughter needs me more than she ever did. And I am glad to be here for her!

**Narrative 2 - What to Do When Your Child Is Diagnosed With Bipolar Disorder – by Letisha Crone**

**Encourage Self-Care In Others**

As the parent of a child with bipolar disorder, it's important to encourage self-care in your child.

This means making sure they get enough sleep, eat a balanced diet, and exercise regularly. It also means teaching them how to cope with stress in healthy ways.

Encouraging self-care in others can be difficult, but it's important to remember that everyone is different and there is no one-size-fits-all approach.

Be patient and understanding, and offer support when needed. If you're struggling to encourage self-care in your child, reach out to a mental health professional for help.

**Engage Others in your child's recovery**

Other people can be vital in your child's recovery from bipolar disorder. Here are a few ways to engage others in your child's care:

1. Educate yourself and others about the illness. In order to help your child, the more you know, the better prepared you will be to do so.

    a. Talk to your child's doctor, read books, and look for online resources. Then, share what you've learned with other family members and friends.

2. Find a support group for families dealing with bipolar disorder. Talking to someone who understands what you're going through can be extremely beneficial.

    a) Sharing your experiences and learning from others can be done in a safe environment provided by these groups.

3. Advocate for your child. Parents have many skills that can benefit their children as they live with bipolar disorder.

    a) You may not be able to change your child's symptoms, but you may be able to ease his or her life by advocating for him or her at school, on social media, and elsewhere.

4. Practice self-care so that you will have the energy and patience needed to take care of a person living with bipolar disorder.

   a) You need sleep, time away from work or school, healthy eating habits (in moderation), time for yourself—anything that helps keep stress levels down and makes you feel good about yourself!

5. Keep an eye out for suicide warning signs. If your child talks about suicide, starts getting isolated, or loses interest in things she cares about before age 18, get help right away.

   a) There is no single way to tell if someone is suicidal; however, some warning signs include:

      i.    Talking Or Writing About Death;

      ii.   Feeling Hopeless;

      iii.  Behaving Recklessly;

      iv.   Withdrawing From Friends And Family;

      v.    Making Comments Such As People Would Be Better Off Without Me;

      vi.   Giving Away Possessions;

      vii.  Experiencing Dramatic Mood Swings;

      viii. Exhibiting Rage Outbursts Followed By Crying Spells And Guilt Feelings Afterward.

6. Teach your child how to handle stressors positively.

   a) Make sure he/she has outlets like physical activity and creative outlets like drawing and painting that allow him to vent frustrations without resorting to aggressive behavior when stressed.

**Narrative 2 - What to Do When Your Child Is Diagnosed With Bipolar Disorder – by Letisha Crone**

## Know when to ask for professional help

As a parent, it can be difficult to know when to seek professional help for your child. If you are noticing signs of mental illness, such as changes in mood, behavior, or sleep patterns, it is important to reach out to a mental health professional. Early intervention is key in mental health recovery.

Your child's mental health provider will be able to diagnose and treat your child. They may also provide support and resources for you as a parent It's crucial to keep in mind that you're not on this journey by yourself. There are many organizations and groups that offer support for families dealing with mental illness. Seek out these resources and connect with other parents who understand what you are going through.

Understand how genetic research can help you better understand your child's illness Researchers are learning more about how bipolar disorder is passed down in families. Studies of identical and fraternal twins have shown that bipolar disorder is more likely to occur in identical twins, who share the same genes, than in fraternal twins, who share only some of the same genes. This suggests that genes play a role in causing bipolar disorder.

If you have a family member with bipolar disorder, you may be worried about your child developing the illness. However, it's important to remember that just because someone has a family member with bipolar disorder does not mean they will develop the illness. In fact, most people with bipolar disorder do not have a family member with the illness.

## The bottom line

If your child has been diagnosed with bipolar disorder, the most important thing you can do is to get them the help they need. This means finding a mental health professional who can provide treatment and support. Also, remember to look after your own well-being at this time.

Make time for self-love and self-care every day. And finally, don't forget that you are not alone. To help you get through this difficult time, there are a wide range of resources and support groups available.

# Narrative 3 - Bipolar Disorder: My Story by Mils Parker

## Narrative 3 - Bipolar Disorder: My Story by Mils Parker

Sincerely, I can say that until the end of college, I showed no outward symptoms of a mental illness. The beginning of it all happened during the final week of my second to last college quarter. I was 23. Before spring break, I still had one final exam to take. I was expected to receive my diploma after spring quarter.

In the civil engineering class, I placed second. I met a classmate at a bar for a pitcher of green beer during finals week. I saw the waitress add the green food coloring to the beer. The remaining events of that day are vague. And not in the sense that I "got drunk and blacked out," but rather in the sense that when I got back to the apartment, my roommate said I looked like I had had thirty beers. Actually, I never even finished the pitcher.

I can still picture the rush of adrenaline and the sensation that my arms were on fire. For the first time in my life, I recall having very trembling hands and feeling extremely anxious. I had a hard time getting through the final because I didn't feel well.

During the return trip from Athens to Canton for spring break, the emotion persisted. I couldn't sit still at all as the anxiety increased and the rush of adrenaline persisted. The thought was going through my head quickly. We arrived back at our house after what seemed like an eternity. I just needed to get home so I could tell my mother what was happening and perhaps go to the hospital emergency room.

When I got home, I was unable to stay still or even sleep. The fear increased. Even sitting down to watch TV was impossible for me. The green beer I drank, according to my mother and her boyfriend, may have been laced. In either case, we were aware that I needed medical attention, so they took me there. While I waited in the crowded waiting area, I vaguely recall shouting religious declarations. I was accepted into the community mental health ward.

I didn't sleep at all for the vast majority of the time I was by myself. I started to experience grandiose paranoid delusions. Maybe I committed a crime I don't remember, and that's why I ended up in this place. My mind began to play mind games with me. Time completely escaped my grasp. It seemed like I had been in that room for weeks.

My doctor and the nurses were the only people I saw for several days. I remember initially refusing the daily medication that they started giving me for the first few days. I reasoned that since drugs had put me in this situation, how could they possibly help me escape? I refused to take my medication when a nurse asked me to do so for the fifth or sixth time. Do you not want to return home, she asked?

Home. Even the definition of "home" escaped my mind. Since my mind had been going 200 miles per hour for about four or five days, I had forgotten that my family and I lived in a house just around the corner from this hospital.

At that point, I started taking the medication, and I gradually started getting better. It was identified at the time as a drug-induced psychotic episode, most likely brought on by consuming beer laced with PCP. According to my doctor, it was probably a "one-time thing."

For almost a year, I took the medications that my doctor had prescribed. I did not return to school in time to graduate in the spring of 2003 as I had originally intended. I had to take a quarter off to mentally recharge.

For my final quarter of undergrad classes, however, I came back in the fall of 2003. My psychiatrist claimed that before I returned, I was doing well enough that he weaned me off of my medications gradually. For better or worse, I was once again medication-free around the time I got back to campus.

I nevertheless completed my final quarter successfully and received a Cum Laude Bachelor of Science in Civil Engineering in November 2003. The following quarter, in winter 2004, I made the decision to attend graduate school for civil engineering as well. I was having a great time and was ecstatic to learn about the engineering research process. It was all brand new to me.

I started to relapse when I started graduate school after being off my medication for a while. Once more, I had trouble sleeping. I started making lofty plans, like creating and building my own home. My racing thoughts started to turn into religious delusions.

During these times, I start to believe that a wide range of illogical ideas are actually true and that it was a mistake for me not to believe this earlier. I recall having a lengthy phone conversation about religion with my best friend.

**Narrative 3 - Bipolar Disorder: My Story by Mils Parker**

Night after night I couldn't sleep, until I finally called my mother in a panic and said something was wrong.

She picked me up, drove me home, and then back to the neighborhood psychiatric ward.

My second episode was worse than the first. I believed I was the antichrist, the messiah, or both. As the messiah/antichrist was being exposed to the entire world in the nearby hospital, I thought the news channels were live-broadcasting me on TV.

I reasoned that everyone who worked at the hospital and watched the news detested me for it. I frequently heard voices, from my professors and classmates to God, in my head.

Once more, I was given medication, and this incident was misdiagnosed as a separate, second psychotic episode. I was compelled to leave graduate school, never completing a quarter.

I continued taking medicine for a lot longer and was even healthy enough to work for an engineering firm for a year and a half.

Then I made the decision to drive to a local graduate program. Even though I was feeling down and unsure of my mental state, it went well.

I completed a 140-page thesis for my master's degree in civil engineering. But once more, a different physician ultimately asserted that I was fine and gradually weaned me off of my medications in May 2008, just before I graduated.

All of this tension led to the onset of my third and most severe manic episode. Despite the fact that I lacked insight, life was moving too quickly for me.

While residing with her, my erratic behavior alarmed my girlfriend. Once more, I had trouble sleeping.

I once got lost while memorizing the route from Cleveland to Canton. I was a bad driver and had a bad car accident.

**Narrative 3 - Bipolar Disorder: My Story by Mils Parker**

On my 27th birthday in December 2008, I was admitted to the neighborhood mental hospital after losing my job in a week, my girlfriend, and my best friend.

This mania attack was a long-lasting one that didn't just happen while I was in the hospital.

A fistfight with my brother, a run-in with Cleveland police, risky behavior, lofty goals, shopping binges, auditory hallucinations, and even seeing things when I closed my eyes, like strobe lights, music visualizers, and even aliens, were all part of it.

I was finally given the medical diagnosis of severe bipolar 1 disorder with psychotic symptoms. In reality, all three of my episodes were severe manic ones with some psychosis.

I was given medication once more, this time for good, and haven't experienced a manic episode in more than four years.

But at this point in my life, I'm looking for more than just staying home by myself and feeling depressed as a result. I consider myself to be very valuable to this world.

I want to see if I can handle the pressure of a part-time job in the future, so I'll be volunteering a little bit. As I meet all requirements and unquestionably have lived experience with mental illness, I'll also be training to become a certified peer supporter in the field of mental health in the near future.

Overall, I want to continue my career and eventually return to the field of civil engineering. With the right coping mechanisms and encouraging people nearby, I've done it before and I know I can do it again.

My realization that I am not alone in my recovery has been helped by support groups. I firmly believe that healing is possible. My story is still unfolding. I'm all set to reclaim my life.

# Narrative 4 - My Bipolar Relationship Maintenance Experiences
## - By Mandy Wallace

**Narrative 4 - My Bipolar relationship maintenance experiences - By Mandy Wallace**

Although communicating with a loved one who suffers from a mental illness can be challenging and frustrating, there are ways to do it. You might not know a lot about your relative's perspective when they're symptomatic.

You can strengthen the foundation of your relationship by using these suggestions.

Recognize that you cannot change your family member; you can only change yourself in order to move forward with them. However, the adjustments you make may enhance your shared lives.

It's essential to learn as much as you can about their illness so you can empathize with whatever struggles they may be experiencing.

**Avoid the Stigma of Belief**

Be honest with yourself about the identity of the person you care about. Even if we are very close to someone who has a mental illness and support his rights, we might also have our own biases and misconceptions about the condition. We must learn to distinguish between an illness and an individual.

**Recognize perplexing behavior.**

It's normal to feel hurt by the symptoms of mental illness because many of them manifest through social behavior. We frequently assume that actions are thought out and planned.

You might be tempted to think that your brother is deliberately trying to embarrass you when, for instance, you invite him to dinner with your friends and feel embarrassed by his constant checking to see if he locked his car.

This may also be how some of his friends and strangers perceive him; stigma has that effect.

It can be difficult to remember the truth—that your relative has a disease and that the behavior is one of his symptoms—when people around you perceive him in this way.

That is a crucial fact to keep in mind, even though it does not justify cruel or violent behavior.

**Review the areas that need improvement.**

You still have the power to make decisions that will help you and your relative's situation. You may decide to work together to improve communication, you may each work to maintain friendships and other supportive relationships.

You may both decide to receive talk therapy from a psychologist. The fact that you have some degree of control over some things doesn't change the fact that the illness is real and not anyone's fault or a flaw in their character.

The degree to which your relative's symptoms are present at any given time will determine her ability to make wise decisions.

**Obtain assistance from others.**

You are aware that your loved one's condition is not everything. You might appreciate her sense of humor, familiarity with your past, listening skills, and advice.

A person with a mental illness might believe that it jeopardizes her identity and self-respect. Your loved one will go through stages of adjusting to the difficulties of her illness, just like anyone else.

She might appear self-absorbed and unable to give others the usual amount of attention and energy during these times.

If you broaden your own support system beyond your relative, both you and she will be better able to handle the situation.

Boost your relationships with your family and friends. This relieves some of the pressure on your relative to assist you as she did prior to becoming ill.

She could use that energy to make progress toward living well.

Getting the necessary social support may also help you feel stronger and less resentful of her.

**Expect Respectful Conduct.**

Making modifications to account for your relative's illness does not eliminate the requirement for fundamental rules and guidelines. Inform your relative of the expectations you have for him in order for you to get along.

Make sure your loved one is aware of the standards you have for him and that you regard him as a whole person.

Your home should be a safe place, and you should have a plan in place for what to do if the safety of a family member or other loved one is in danger.

These are two of the most crucial requirements. Prepare your family and yourself to deal with emergencies. Share with your relative your expectations for daily life.

For instance, tell your father that if he starts yelling at you, you won't engage in further conversation. To have more fruitful discussions with your relative, use the communication advice provided below.

**Develop your communication skills.**

All of your relationships will benefit from improved communication, but those involving mental illness require it even more. Building good habits is a key component of effective communication.

You can make decisions that increase your likelihood of achieving your goals. Perhaps you want to be able to tell your granddaughter to take a shower without starting a fight or tell your husband that you are concerned about his smoking without getting the cold shoulder.

The use of statements that express your perspective rather than imposing a perceived behavior is a very effective strategy for dealing with this.

Instead of saying "You're not listening," try saying "I am concerned because you don't seem interested in what I'm saying."

You can get closer to your goals by making deliberate changes to the way you communicate.

**Consider it from their angle.**

Do your best to learn as much as you can about the illness and experiences of your relative. They may see things differently than you think because of their symptoms. They might be struggling with strong emotions like fear, low self-esteem, delusions, or hallucinations. Even if they don't express it, all of this might be happening.

Try to put yourself in their position and consider their feelings as opposed to just what they are saying. Respecting them and their potential experiences will help you communicate more effectively and increase the likelihood that they will truly hear and comprehend you.

Give your friend or relative the benefit of the doubt by first assuming that the issue is not that they are not motivated to change, but rather that they are not yet able, if they have done something that bothers you.

It can be tempting to think that the other person is being difficult on purpose. Even if your loved one dislikes cleaning up, she probably has the best of intentions. Even though she is aware that she needs to clean, she becomes distracted in the heat of the moment and forgets.

Ask her if there is anything that makes cleaning more difficult for her. Would a note on the refrigerator or kitchen door be helpful if she simply forgets? What should the sign say, in her opinion? Ask her for suggestions so that you can work together on something.

You'll see that in this instance, you're still able to convey the essence of your emotions: you're angry about the other person's behavior and you want them to act differently so that you can feel better.

This method of communication is more likely to get you both what you want and is less likely to fuel resentment—both of yours and theirs.

# Narrative 4 - My Bipolar relationship maintenance experiences - By Mandy Wallace

## Concentrate on your bigger goals.

Try to keep in mind what your true, long-term goal is whenever you are upset. It might be to maintain harmony with your spouse or to motivate your kid to eat healthier. Getting them to understand how much you put up with for their benefit is probably not your true objective, but when we're upset, we can become defensive.

Start a conversation as soon as possible after an upsetting event, but after you've had some time to collect your thoughts and speak calmly. Recent events will be more likely to bring you together, and you won't allow irritations to fester and turn into resentment. In order to achieve your larger goals, you must effectively communicate your most significant emotions, not bury them.

## Use language that is clear, simple, and direct.

Start the conversation off right to make it more fruitful. First, get the person's attention by asking, "Can I speak with you?" Discuss one subject at a time and give brief updates ("I want to talk about tonight's dinner") Express your thoughts clearly ("I miss cooking with you guys; it's been a while. Instead of implying ("You never do anything with me anymore," or "Would you help me make dinner tonight?"), ask directly.

## Specify what you desire and why.

In most cases, you can agree on the facts of the situation if you state them (for example, "These forms are due back to your school tomorrow, and you haven't filled them out."). Describe the action you want the other person to take in detail and how it would make you feel if they did it ("Please read and sign them before we have lunch. If they were finished, I'd be relieved, and we could enjoy the rest of the afternoon knowing that you were prepared for school.

Explicitly describing a successful outcome can be very inspiring. For instance, you might say that you'd be grateful for their assistance in taking out the trash or that you'd be delighted to be spending time with them if they came along for a walk with you.

Ask the person for ideas on how to make things better; if they helped develop the concept, they'll be more willing to try it.

# Narrative 5 - Learning How to Support Your Family and Child By Anonymous Mother

**Narrative 5 - Learning How to Support Your Family and Child By Anonymous Mother**

Although raising a child with a mental illness can be difficult, there are steps you can take to ease your burden.

Start by observing your kids' emotions, behaviors, and moods. Early intervention is essential because mental health conditions frequently worsen if left untreated, especially when there are signs of psychosis.

Many diseases have cyclical patterns, and intense symptomatic periods may come and go. Sometimes symptoms aren't even obvious.

Children may conceal some symptoms by acting and speaking in ways they think are expected of them.

**How to Respond If You Observe Symptoms**

If you believe you have symptoms, make an appointment as soon as possible with a qualified psychiatrist or psychologist; if that is not possible, then see your child's pediatrician or primary care doctor.

Make sure to give your healthcare provider as much thorough information as you are able to:

- Past assessments of mental health and other medical records.
- Symptoms' descriptions, when they first appeared, and whether or not they have changed over time.
- Any prescription drugs or other treatments your child is receiving for a health condition.
- Anything else that is required or that you feel could provide useful details.

You should inquire about their reasoning if a doctor, psychologist, or counselor refuses to make a diagnosis or refer you to another specialist.

Trust your instincts and seek a second opinion when in doubt. Being cautious is frequently preferable to ignoring a potentially serious issue.

You should seek medical attention right away if your child reports hearing or seeing things that aren't there without the use of drugs or alcohol.

**Narrative 5 - Learning How to Support Your Family and Child By Anonymous Mother**

This could be a psychotic episode. These episodes may also include irrational and paranoid claims, denial of reality, removing clothing, reckless and dangerous behavior, or assertions of invincibility and other superhuman abilities.

Even though there are many different treatment options, it can be challenging to find and obtain the right care. Psychology Today and SAMHSA both have directories of mental health specialists and treatment centers.

**How To Keep Aiding Your Child In Learning Everything You Can**

In addition to seeking medical assistance, you should educate yourself as much as you can about your child's mental health condition.

Consult the school for your child. Verify that your child is getting the right support and services at school. Without support, children with mental health issues might struggle in school, which can cause frustration and stress.

Thankfully, the law mandates that schools offer unique services and accommodations to students with mental health conditions that affect their ability to learn. Learn more about how to obtain the services you need for education.

**Exercise Your Child**

Even if everything seems to be working against you, you must continue to be respectful of and sympathetic to your child's feelings. You shouldn't get upset with them for actions that are out of their control.

This does not preclude you from establishing boundaries or enforcing rules. It does imply, however, that you must consider your child's mental health when determining your expectations. This is frequently mentioned as a step in "finding a new normal."

People who experience mental health conditions might never be the same as they were before, despite the fact that this can be difficult to accept.

Everyone will experience frustration and stress if we hold people to the same standards of conduct as they did before their mental health condition developed.

## How to Maintain Family Cohesion

When you have a mentally ill child, it is easy to let your worry about them take over your life. Keep in mind the following:

### Self-care is important.

It is your duty to look after and provide for your child, but it is also your duty to look after yourself. You may need to change your priorities or way of life, but you shouldn't let the difficulties brought on by your child's mental illness cause you to neglect other significant aspects of your life.

In some circumstances, the strain of raising a child with a mental illness can worsen a parent's mental health issues.

Do not hesitate to seek help for yourself if you start to feel as though you are struggling with depression or anxiety.

Maintaining your own mental health will make you a good role model for your child and keep you healthy and able to look after them.

### Look after your family.

Keep in mind that if you have other kids, they might feel neglected if all the focus is on their sibling's mental health issues.

Spend time with each of them to ensure that they are aware of what their siblings are experiencing.

Maintaining a harmonious and balanced family can be very beneficial in lowering stress levels for everyone, which can help lessen mental illness symptoms.

### Activate Your Family

If you share a home with a partner or spouse, or if you have other children, try to involve them in being an advocate for your child.

Although you might approach problems and obstacles in a different way than they do, you should still find ways to combine your strengths to make up for any weaknesses.

**Narrative 5 - Learning How to Support Your Family and Child By Anonymous Mother**

Prepare to compromise, pay attention, and be receptive to new ideas.

You might find that some family members are not very interested in helping you and your child deal with the difficulties brought on by your child's mental health condition.

Additionally, a spouse or significant other might have a negative impact on your child.

They might demand punishment for actions your child is unable to control, reject the existence of any issues, or insist on an unreasonable course of action.

Assuming that everyone, including yourself, will always respond in the best way is unrealistic when helping to raise a child who has a mental health condition.

But you must also understand that it is your duty to safeguard your child, even from people you care about.

# Narrative 6 - Through my eyes: My battle with bipolar
## By Linda Franks

## Narrative 6 - Through my eyes: My battle with bipolar By Linda Franks

"Her eyes are blue". My father's first words to me after I was born. His eyes were blue. The idea that he was looking for something we shared right away when he first saw me makes me incredibly sad.

All newborns have blue eyes, but mine changed to hazel. My dad never realized that we actually did share a characteristic while he was still alive. *Our bipolar disorders were mutual.*

My mother informed me as a child that my dad suffered from "manic depression." That made me think of a pot of boiling water whose lid was vibrating and steam was escaping, ready to burst at any second.

My father used to buy expensive stereo equipment and Rolex watches for thousands of dollars before locking himself in his bedroom for days at a time. He used to lovingly tease me until I was laughing on one day, then he would suddenly snap at me in a furious manner the following day.

His outbursts made me feel very afraid. I spent all of my energy attempting to understand why he did what he did, always taking it personally. I was the girl who struggled with father issues, which were complicated by untreated bipolar disorder.

I had bipolar disorder as a child, but I was always a people person. My first word was "hi," not "mama" or "dada." As soon as I could, I introduced myself to everyone I encountered.

I had a hard time sitting still in elementary school because I was so hyperactively energetic. Because I talked too much in class, my teachers frequently sent me to the principal's office. I crammed so many social and extracurricular events into my high school schedule that I hardly had time for homework.

I worked a job and had a busy schedule of classes in college, but I also immersed myself in activist organizations and went out every night of the week. I had more affairs than I could count and was always making new friends.

My thoughts would quickly shift from one topic to the next. I swung back and forth based on my emotions. I switched around in my sexual identities, residences, jobs, and relationships. I was a passenger on a locomotive that was speeding along at 120 mph and showing no signs of slowing down.

## Narrative 6 - Through my eyes: My battle with bipolar By Linda Franks

My mom and dad split up during my senior year of college. He had purchased firearms and had been shooting holes in the ground. He would spend hours driving to distant, cheap motels before calling her and threatening to commit suicide. He had his stomach pumped and was taking pills.

My mother's work clothes shrank after being washed, dried, and hung back up on the same hangers. I saw tiny doll-sized suits that were wrinkled and disfigured beyond recognition, with my father—a psychotic lunatic—standing over them.

**The breaking news that altered everything.**

My mother came to the punk clothing store where I worked to tell me that my dad had just committed suicide. I was restocking neon red lipstick at the time. I was numb for four years after his passing before I finally lost it. I experienced my first major depressive episode around this time. I took a leave of absence from work due to my total inability to function.

My mother sent me for a psychological evaluation, and I came home with a nine-page report after six hours of testing. In black and white, it was there. *Bipolar II was the official diagnosis for me.*

When I discovered I had my father's illness, I was horrified. Would I ultimately commit suicide as well? A bipolar diagnosis appeared to be a death warrant at the time.

I started going to see a psychiatrist and a therapist. I experimented with mood stabilizers, antipsychotics, anticonvulsants, and antidepressants. I had a difficult time maintaining chemical balance in my brain, but I eventually discovered a combination of medications that lessened the ferocity of my mood swings.

**Experiencing a crisis in life.**

I got married for the second time in 2002. My husband was a tyrannical, violent man. I had been hauling tons of concrete and cast iron, tearing out the kitchen and bathroom, and meeting with dozens of contractors as we renovated our home. It was a very stressful situation. I was agitated and irritable, and everything that went slightly wrong in my racing mind was being catastrophized.

I downed a bunch of pills with a balloon glass of $6 Merlot from the gas station after a nasty argument with my husband. I attempted suicide when I was 32 years old, bipolar, and bipolar. Like my father, who suffered from bipolar disorder, 65 years ago.

Why did I do that? I knew that this would kill my mother because I was the only child, but I was under the influence of mania.

I ended up in the emergency room strapped to a stretcher. Every half hour or so, I would experience a seizure, and as reality hit me, I would go in and out of consciousness while kicking and pulling at my restraints.

I transferred from there to an inpatient mental hospital late at night, where the staff led me to the room I would share with a roommate who had just been released from prison.

The following two nights, I couldn't sleep because of the numerous lights that were always on and the woman with schizophrenia down the hall. She stole everyone's jeans during the day and kept them stacked in her closet. She would pace incoherently down the echoing hallway at night, screaming both sides of an argument with herself.

I maintained my composure and demonstrated that I was healthy enough to be released after only three days. I vowed to keep my word and never return.

**Recognizing my illness.**

I'll never forget my mother's expression in the emergency room. Despite the fact that I should have known better, I made her go through the same thing that my father did.

Bipolar disorder does is that. It causes you to lose perspective, focusing your attention on a small area to the point where everything and everyone else is lost in the background. It is utterly self-absorbed.

As I began to feel better, I became aware of how serious my condition actually was. Without proper treatment, this mood disorder may be fatal. I can now see that I could experience what happened to my father.

**Narrative 6 - Through my eyes: My battle with bipolar By Linda Franks**

I am constantly anticipating what will happen next.

I am aware of what occurs when I neglect my health and give in to the voices that urge me to skip meals or sleep past my usual bedtime.

Any minor setback can cause the whispering voice in my head to start speaking, so I need to be extra careful when something goes wrong in my life.

The voice that claims I can leave by passing away. I don't want to have the same fate as my father, who must have heard the same voice.

Ironically, it took my father's passing for me to fully comprehend him. My bipolar disorder was first identified as a result of my response to his suicide.

I was able to make some sense of my dad's actions by accepting my diagnosis because I understood that they were neither his nor my fault.

I now understand that engaging in shoplifting solely for the high, sharing beds with a large number of strangers, and making suicide attempts with alcohol and pills were all signs of my mental illness.

The same thing was happening behind my dad's outbursts, impatience, annoyance, and even suicide. It just had a different face.

I am reminded of this ongoing insight by flashes of both his and my actions, which helped me to make sense of all the unsettling memories of my father and the things I learned. My diagnosis taught me how to comprehend and pardon myself as well as my father.

**Current situation.**

I am currently penning a book called My Daddy: A Narrative about my experiences as a survivor and advocate. By sharing my experience, I hope to inspire hope in the millions of people who have been impacted by suicide and bipolar disorder.

**Narrative 6 - Through my eyes: My battle with bipolar By Linda Franks**

I have persevered through several significant manic and depressive episodes and emerged unscathed.

Additionally, I have discovered a brand-new confidence, one that is grounded in a genuine sense of self-acceptance rather than the fanciful, intoxicating delusions of a manic mind.

I constantly struggle, particularly when I have seductive hypomania, but I just try my best and try to set reasonable boundaries for myself.

I was once asked if I would be willing to cure my bipolar disorder. No, is my response.

My past has shaped me into the person I am today, and no matter how I got here—whether it was because of my bipolar disorder or my personality—I am proud of who

I am now. I am living proof that a bipolar diagnosis does not spell the end of a person's life. I've thrived, not just managed to survive.

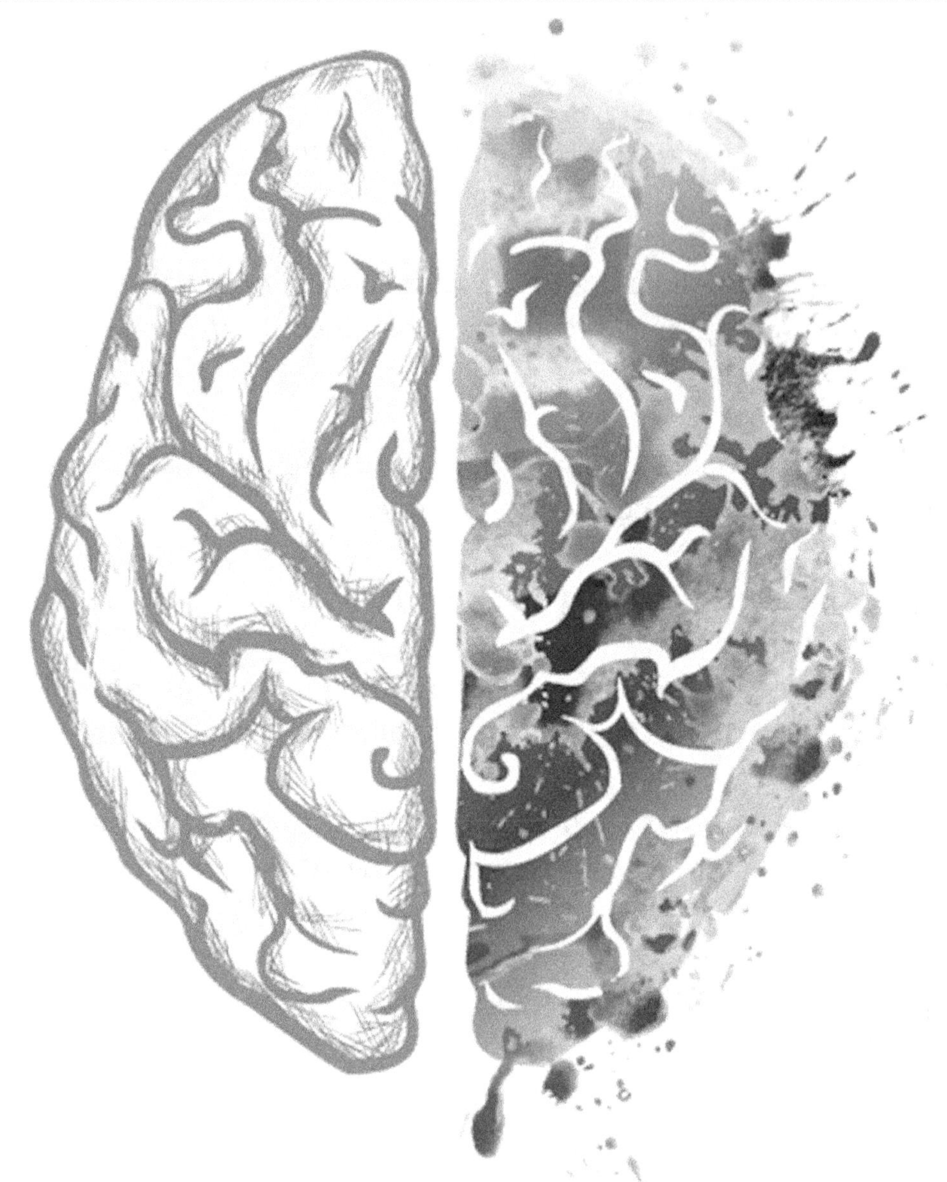

# Narrative 7 - Fray's Experience With Bipolar Disorder

# Narrative 7 - Fray's experience with bipolar disorder

I have personal experience with bipolar disorder, I was diagnosed with bipolar 1 (the most severe form of the mood disorder) as an inpatient at the the Lambeth Hospital in south London, when I was just 11 years old. I am now 39.

Being diagnosed at such a young age was difficult, and I had no idea what my future held. Due to three episodes of illness—mania, depression, and psychosis—in one year, which caused me to lose consciousness, I was hospitalized.

Bipolar disorder is a severe mental illness that alters mood states to either extreme manic highs or crippling depressive lows, with periods of normal functioning in between episodes.

As someone who has this, I have also gone through psychosis during mania, which necessitates immediate hospitalization because my mind becomes wildly out of control. I was admitted to the hospital for my bipolar disorder twice (in 1998 and 2005), both times because of a severe episode of mania and psychosis.

I was depressed, anxious, afraid, and vulnerable when I was a teenager in the hospital. I falsely believed that I had been sexually abused, and this false belief became the foundation of my reality (delusions).

The doctors were able to restore my health to full function by starting me on new medication (mood stabilizers) and giving me anti-psychotics to help me recover from my manic episode.

In addition, over the course of four months, I received individual therapy, participated in group therapy with other teenagers in the adolescent unit, and received support from an outstanding team of nurses and a psychiatrist who thought I could recover. Once my mind had stabilized, I eventually returned home and began a protracted process of counseling and recovery.

I was able to attend college, earn my degrees, travel, meet people, go on dates, and live my life. But in 2012, as a result of some stressors in my life, I started to suffer from depression that included suicidal thoughts.

We think the reason it was so frightening was because my medication, carbamazepine, stopped working as I grew older.

## Narrative 7 - Fray's experience with bipolar disorder

I participated in group therapy with other teenagers and had the support of an outstanding nursing staff and a psychiatrist who thought I could recover.

This kind of depression is very challenging to manage. Most days, I didn't leave my bed until I ate.

I lacked the willpower, hope, and motivation to stand up. I lacked motivation and was unable to handle life.

I hardly ever spoke to friends or did laundry. Fortunately, I told my family and medical team about this because I was afraid of having suicidal thoughts. I just wanted to get away from the pain my mind was in without taking any action.

Unfortunately, a few months later, the depression developed into a manic episode, possibly as a result of my mood stabilizer's failure to work and the antidepressants I was taking.

Bipolar sufferers are always at risk for experiencing drug-induced intoxication.

My libido was high, I was agitated, talking quickly, and I was exposed as a result. My mind then began to falsely believe that I was being held by a criminal gang that my family was running when the psychosis first began. It was extremely frightful.

They attempted to restore my mood and mental clarity by sectioning me, treating me with medication once more, and having me participate in therapy in the hospital over a period of months.

My lifeline was starting to take lithium, a medication that has been able to stabilize my mood for the past five years.

My father has bipolar disorder, which suggests that there may be a biological basis for this, though research is still in its infancy.

Since 2017, I have not gone through a mania or severe depression episode, but I am aware that since bipolar disorder is a chronic condition, it might happen again in the future.

## Narrative 7 - Fray's experience with bipolar disorder

Many mental illnesses begin in childhood or adolescence as a result of a person's upbringing, their environment, or a genetic predisposition.

It is crucial that parents, guardians, and teachers keep an eye out for symptoms of bipolar disorder, anxiety, depression, and self-harm.

It is crucial to take a child to the doctor and request a referral to psychiatry if you believe they have experienced a manic or hypomanic episode and are also depressed.

I wouldn't be here today if it weren't for the help of my parents and doctors.

I hope we can emphasize the importance of providing support to people of all ages who are dealing with mental illness.

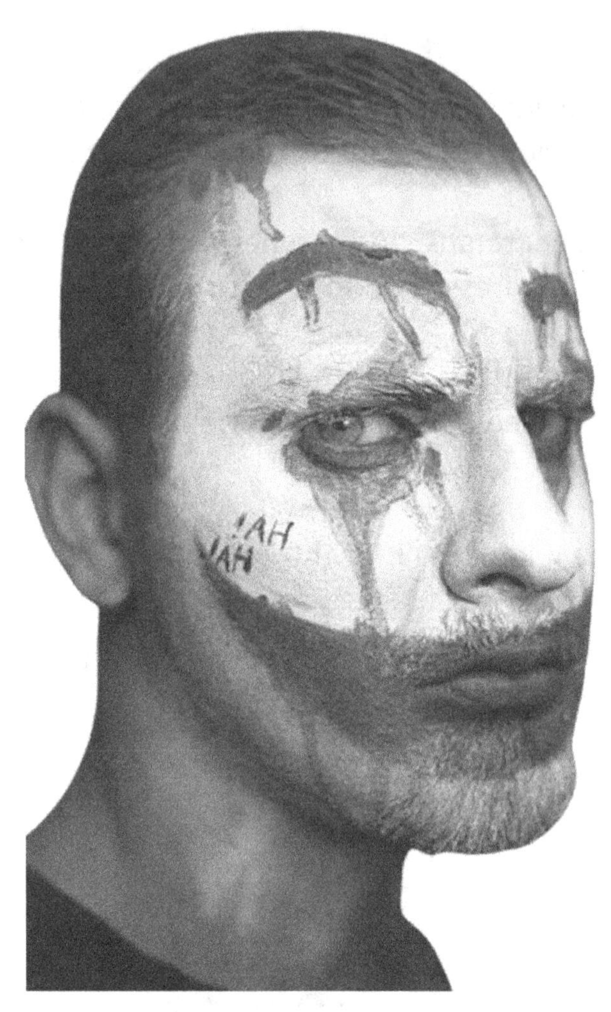

# Narrative 8 - A True Story About Bipolar Disorder By Ricky Manning's Wife.

We frequently hear about how a mental illness can alter a person's life, but do we really know how much?

*But did you know that a mental illness could result in losing your job, your family, or even going to jail?*

All those things can be caused by mental illness, including bipolar disorder, as Ricky can vouch for.

His story begins with the past experiences of members of his immediate family.

His grand father and sister-in-law were both Holocaust survivors, two people who had actually gone through one of the most traumatic experiences a person could go through.

Both Ricky's mother and grandmother experienced severe depressive episodes, and it's possible that his grandmother also had bipolar disorder.

When she was 70, Ricky's mother also started to show signs of Parkinson's disease. Ricky believed he had inherited his problems because of his family's history of mental illness.

One of the risk factors for anxiety, along with brain chemistry, personality, and life events, is genetics. The biggest risk factor for bipolar disorder is also family history. In addition, Ricky is an Sephardic Jew, a group known to have a genetic predisposition to bipolar disorder.

**The Devastating Effects of Mental Illness**

Ricky was a happy and sociable child who did not exhibit any symptoms of mental illness at that age. But as the years went by, Ricky's struggles with school and deadlines overwhelmed him, and he started to experience anxiety and trouble sleeping.

Although his parents supported him, he was unable to seek out professional assistance.

## Narrative 8 - A True Story About Bipolar Disorder By Ricky Manning's Wife.

As he grew older, Ricky's sleep habits deteriorated, and he started getting an average of four hours per night.

He found sleep aids to be helpful, but they made him tired the next day and were addictive. The valium eventually lost its effect, and the insomnia returned.

Ricky was a successful dermatologist who ran a residency program and operated three to four times per week despite getting little sleep.

However, after turning 38, Ricky experienced a manic episode that lasted 3–4 months, followed by a depressive phase. After a brief course of mood stabilizers, he was eventually kept on antidepressants and anxiety medications.

People with bipolar disorder may experience episodes that are classified as either:

- An abnormally high, expansive, or irritable mood accompanied by excessive energy.
- Or activity that seriously impairs functioning is referred to as a manic episode.
- Similar to a manic episode but not severe enough to result in significant social or professional problems.

A major depressive episode is characterized by a protracted depressed state or a loss of interest or pleasure. Manic and major depressive symptoms are both present in a mixed state. Ricky's anxiety and bipolar symptoms grew over the ensuing years.

There are numerous bipolar disorder symptoms, which may include:
- Sadness
- Feelings of guilt or worthlessness
- Loss of enthusiasm for once-enjoyable activities.
- Fatigue or a decrease in energy.
- Weight change of a significant magnitude.
- Complaining of discomfort.
- Thoughts or plans of suicide.

Ricky lost patience with his more challenging patients and started verbally abusing his wife, but he was still successful as a specialist dermatologist with an international group.

### Narrative 8 - A True Story About Bipolar Disorder By Ricky Manning's Wife.

He started to experience hand tremors, early Parkinson's disease symptoms, and cataracts, and he required knee replacement surgery during this time. Ricky's physical problems began to worsen, and this led to a serious depression.

New problems require a new physician and new medications. He was able to control his depression thanks to new medications, but he lost his job, he went into a manic phase. Ricky remembers that he "became out of control at this point in my life."

Although Ricky had no control over his extreme mood swings, his mental health issues had taken over his life to the point where it was too much for his family, who had reached their breaking point.

He was Baker Acted by his wife, allowing for a forced evaluation of his mental state.

Ricky was further pushed down a destructive path, despite the fact that this was intended to help him. He battered his wife at home while blaming her for his problems.

Ricky was detained for eight months after he resisted the attack and managed to escape. Ricky discovered Boca Recovery Center in Florida while he was incarcerated, and that is when his life began to turn around.

I was aware that it wasn't me at the time, Ricky remarked. It was both bipolar disorder and depression.

I should have sought help, but instead I vented my frustrations on my family, and I had to pay the price. Boca Recovery Center enabled me to change my life.

Now that Ricky's condition was known, The treatment for bipolar disorder that is most frequently used is cognitive behavioral therapy (CBT).

This evidence-based, solution-focused treatment strategy places a strong emphasis on altering behavior by using particular skills. CBT focuses on how cognition, emotions, and behavior are interconnected and how altering how one thinks about a situation can alter how one behaves.

**Narrative 8 - A True Story About Bipolar Disorder By Ricky Manning's Wife.**

Ricky was in the Boca Recovery Center program for three months before spending a further three months at Osceola House, a transitional living facility for clients who have left the residential level of care.

When Ricky arrived at Boca Recovery Center, he recalled feeling "shackled and put in a van after leaving prison." I was afraid because it was dark. People spoke to me in a human-like manner. They spoke to me as though I mattered and that I was important.

Ricky was in a therapeutic setting that not only addressed his current issue but also the underlying disorder that was fueling it.

Jerry Krims, Ricky's primary therapist, had a profound effect on him by teaching him that he was in a safe environment and that he could express his emotions.

Ricky discovered that his emotions were okay, and he was able to start living a life free of his disorder.

Ricky's treatment team used a thorough strategy to address the problems he was having every day and gave him the tools he needed to maintain long-term recovery.

Ricky also credits his roommate with helping him succeed. "My roommate was a ship captain, and I remember thinking, 'This guy has an important job and a mental illness,'" Ricky recalls. I can accomplish this if he can, too. We had wonderful conversations, and I remember thinking how lucky I was to be in our room together," he said."

**Homecoming Following Treatment**

After finishing his treatment, Ricky went back home and is now content to take each day as it comes. Sadly, the loss of his job, family, freedom, and friends has taught him the harsh reality of living with a mental illness.

I've lived a remarkable life and contributed significantly to society. People don't understand when you have a mental illness, and some friends stop hanging out with you. Some of my relatives have stopped talking to me or my wife.

## Narrative 8 - A True Story About Bipolar Disorder By Ricky Manning's Wife.

Even though it hurts, I try to comprehend. I don't think back because things could have been worse.

Consider the future and creating a life for yourself. I am slowly coming across individuals who accept me.

In addition to taking charge of his life, he avoids caffeine, alcohol, and other drugs while attending the gym almost daily.

He regularly attends support groups. Ricky continues to work on his recovery by telling his story, leading discussions, and helping those who experience similar problems.

He doesn't dwell on the past and keeps looking forward. He values how far he has come, is more committed to his family, and loves his wife more now than ever before.

# Narrative 9 - Being a Single Mom with Bipolar
## by Gwen Halim

One of the most difficult things a person can do is be a single parent.

Not only are you responsible for maintaining a home, paying bills, and balancing a budget in order to survive, but you also have to do so while raising another person who regards you as the center of the universe.

You must lead by example, be strong, assist your child in learning, and prioritize his or her needs.

Bipolar disorder is also one of the most difficult conditions to deal with. Every day, you wake up with a battle between good and evil inside of you.

Some days are better than others. You notice that you are smiling, happy, and at peace. On other days, however, simply getting out of bed is your greatest accomplishment.

Depression can be crippling at times. You feel helpless, worthless, and insignificant. The darkness seems to last forever, and there isn't a single bright spot to make things bearable.

**Combine the two now.**

Being a single parent with bipolar disorder has been something I've struggled with for the past eight years.

There are days when I don't want to live, but I have to. There are days when I just want to cry in bed, but I can't.

I need to get out of bed, fight the monsters, hold back the tears, and go to work so that I can pay for my daughter's music lessons and school lunches. I can't show her my pain.

**Finding a happy medium has never been easy.**

I get out of bed every morning because of her. On some days, I feel as if the world has crumbled around me. I feel as if I'm being attacked, and I'm so stressed that I can't sleep.

Those are usually the days when she refuses to get out of bed without my help. Then she decides to take a 45-minute shower, forcing me to rush out the door in order to get her to school on time.

On nights when she has cheerleading practice after school, I take that hour or two to sit in my car alone and cry.

She can't see me crumble. I never want her to witness my struggle with this disorder.

I believe it is critical that she has a strong female role model, and that person must be me. I've reached out to friends and family, sought professional therapy, and taken medication, but nothing has worked.

Every day, the waves come in.

Some days, on the good days, the waves are small and manageable. I'm content and in control. I have plenty of energy.

The world seems to be at my fingertips.. I am the mother of the year, and I am content. On other days, I'm drowning in a tsunami.

People who are not affected by this have a difficult time grasping and comprehending the feelings.

I've been told numerous times that life is difficult and that I just have to deal with it. Everyone has difficulties and problems.

They don't realize that as a single parent, you don't have the time to process your emotions.

You don't have anyone to assist you in relieving stress, running errands, or paying bills.

Everything is on you.

The weight of the world is on your shoulders, and it can be crushing at times.

Aside from the stresses of everyday life, your brain is telling you that you are worthless.

The battle with this is an ongoing one.

Reach out to anyone you know who is in this situation.

Be the light they didn't realize they needed. Your kind words may be the only reason they are happy today.

It might determine a person's fate and determine whether they live or die.

I've had dark thoughts and feelings many times, but knowing my daughter needs me keeps any actions at bay.

She is my beacon and my light. I must be her pillar of strength.

Be brave and fight. People are looking up to you.

I promise you, no matter how bleak the outlook appears, you will get through it.

Things do not remain dark indefinitely.

# Narrative 10 - What It's Like to Live with Mental Illness: A Day in the Life of a Bipolar Disorder by Carri Philips.

# Narrative 10 - What It's Like to Live with Mental Illness: A Day in the Life of a Bipolar Disorder by Carri Philips.

I can't get out of bed when I wake up. A pink bear seems to be lying across me. Even though all I want to do is sleep, I push myself to get up. This has been the situation for a few days.

Every morning feels like an uphill struggle just to get out of bed. I've had bipolar disorder for as long as I can remember, though I didn't receive an official diagnosis until 2001.

While many days are bad, some days are good. Often, there is a middle ground. Every day is like riding a roller coaster, and occasionally those roller coasters catch fire.

Although the best part of the ride never ends, the worst part always does. My best days are when I feel energized. Not full-blown mania, but the moments when I believe I am capable of contributing to society.

On those better days, pushing myself too far can set off a manic episode, at which point I'm unstoppable. There are no obstacles. I can't stay still because I'm overcome with a wave of creative inspiration.

I sometimes think I could fight both the Batman and Captain America at once.

However, manic behavior always has a cost. Higher highs result in deeper longer falls.

And then there are the bad days. On days like these, I find it difficult to get dressed and can barely move. I want to give up and ball up until the size of a foot ball.

There is no getting out of bed, taking a shower, or dressing. Maybe I won't even eat. Unpredictability is one of the hardest aspects of bipolar disorder. It's impossible to predict when a good day will turn bad or how long a bad day will last. It's a guessing game that never ends well.

**Family and friends.**

Bipolar disorder can strain friendships and family ties. Those around you are affected by your mood, whether it's irritable, ecstatic, or depressed. Your unpredictable nature may annoy you, but it scares those who care about you.

**Narrative 10 - What It's Like to Live with Mental Illness: A Day in the Life of a Bipolar Disorder by Carri Philips.**

There are some days when I keep to myself. I mute the phone and decline to open the door for the visitor. I like to tell myself that I'm protecting other people, but the truth is that it's the only world in which I can function. Any contact with the outside world is too much on those days.
Even the idea of adding another person to the mix hurts because the noise in my head is so loud.

Some of your friends may find it difficult to understand why you need to change plans or spend time alone. They might try to pressure you or make a walk-away threat.

It's best, in my opinion, to let them go. Don't let anyone minimize your mental illness; it is not something you are making up.

**Work**

One of the fortunate ones is me. I have high functioning bipolar, so most weeks I am able to work a full-time schedule.

I took almost a year off of work twice because it took me a while to get used to having bipolar disorder and taking medication. The fact that it gave me time to recover made it the right decision.

You must be careful to maintain a healthy work-life balance. Bipolar disorder will make you want to work nonstop one week and unable to accomplish anything the following.

A four-day work week is ideal for me. It provides me with three days each week to refresh my mental state and get ready for the days ahead. If you are unable to work for a while, it's okay.

Take advantage of whatever is available to you; most communities have assistance programs. If you can work, I think it keeps me stable, so if you can, work. If you are unable to, consider setting a goal in its place.

**How to Help**

Not everything is bad news. You can take steps to improve your chances of experiencing better days.

These are the first three.

1. Sleep –
   a) Get enough rest first. I am aware that this is easier said than done. Getting at least eight hours of sleep, however, will help you maintain your mood and give you more energy to deal with the bad days if you can manage it.
   b) Establishing a regular sleep schedule, abstaining from caffeine and alcohol before bed, and developing a relaxing bedtime routine are all ways to improve your sleep habits.
   c) The more routines you can establish, the better, because the bipolar brain seems to function best with them.

2. 2. Meds and Diet –
   a) Next, eat a balanced diet. I'll say it again: it's easier said than done. At the end of the day, I'm the one who first grabs the bag of Cheetos.
   b) However, consuming healthy foods will bolster both your body and mind. The increased strength makes it simpler to handle the highs and lows of bipolar disorder.
   c) You'll feel better if you eat fresh fruits and vegetables instead of a bag of chips or a box of doughnuts. I frequently demonstrate this theory.
   d) You must take your medications consistently at or about the same time each day. You will battle it for many days.
   e) Every time I have to take a pill, it's a struggle for me, but I keep telling myself how much better my life is when I'm stable.
   f) My medications hold the key to my stability the most. Take your colorful pills if not for you then for the people you care about.

3. 3. Exercise –
   a) Do regular exercise, lastly. Endorphins, which improve mood, are released during exercise. When you're having a bad day, even a quick walk around the block can help.
   b) Exercise outside has the biggest effect on me, but that's not always an option. The aim is to spend at least 30 minutes, three or four times per week, on cleaning.
   c) Exercise also enhances the quality of sleep. A weary body rests more easily.
   d) Just be careful not to overdo it with the exercise. Bipolar disorder sufferers must walk a fine line, so keep track of your reactions to each activity.
   e) Long-term intense exercise can cause mania, so start slowly and with activities that have less impact.
   f) Walking is a simple exercise that is perfect for beginners.

**Narrative 10 - What It's Like to Live with Mental Illness: A Day in the Life of a Bipolar Disorder by Carri Philips.**

**More Advice**

Although bipolar disorder is a difficult illness to manage, there are ways to make it simpler. These are just a few of the things that make my days easier.

- Additionally, there are advantages to doing things like journaling, meditating, and engaging in acts of mindfulness and gratitude.
- I also maintain my mental clarity by aiming for positivity.
- One of the best strategies for maintaining good mental health is to keep your thoughts on positive things.

**Not Alone**

Bear in mind that you are not acting alone. There are people out there who can support and advise you because they are experiencing what you are. When you need to, get in touch with them, and do your best to look after yourself.

I hope that this has provided you with a brief overview of what it's like to have bipolar disorder. Even though managing the condition can be challenging, it is possible.

I will not give up. Even on the days when my mental illness tries to suffocate my life, I fight it every day.

I have bipolar disorder, but it does not make me who I am.

Be resolute to fight on regardless of the circumstances. You'll have difficult days, but you'll get through them.

You'll find that you have fewer bad days if you put the above advice into practice on your better days.

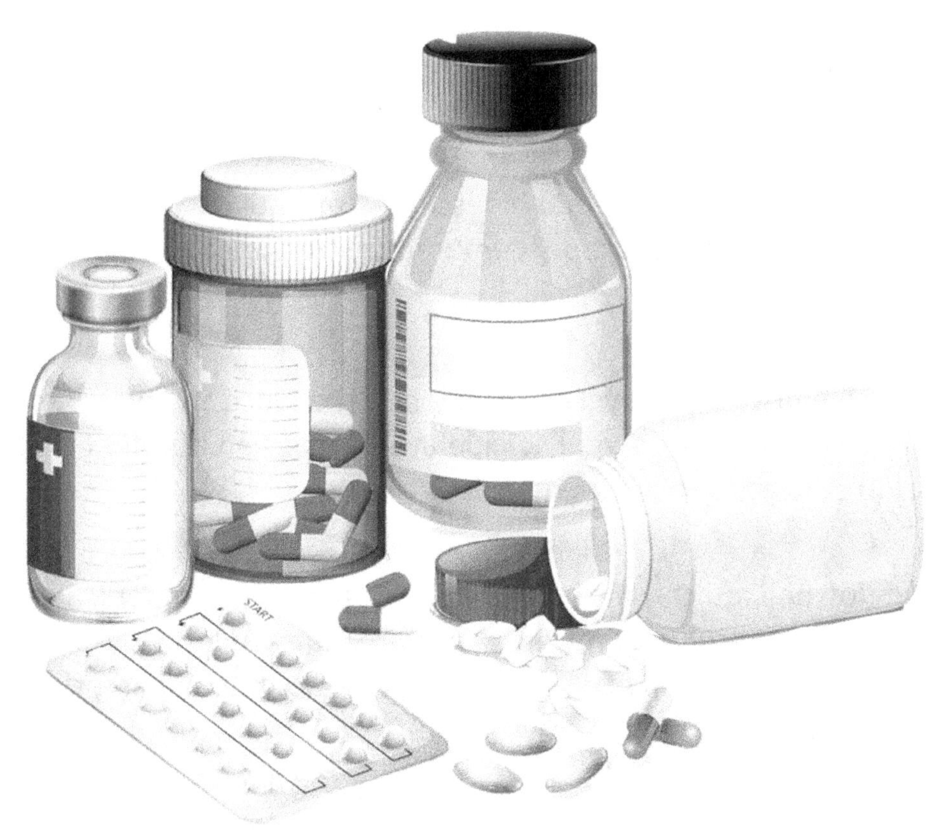

# Narrative 11 - Bipolar Disorder, Dissociative Disorder, and PTSD Recovery – by Joanna's Story

## Narrative 11 - Bipolar disorder, dissociative disorder, and PTSD recovery – by Joanna's Story

Unfortunately, having multiple mental illnesses is not unusual in people. Bipolar disorder, dissociative disorder, and post-traumatic stress disorder are all present in Joanna (PTSD).

Joanna calls her life prior to recovery a "living hell" because she was frequently in and out of the hospital and made several suicide attempts. Even her doctors predicted that she wouldn't always survive the night.

I started going downhill quickly at the age of 22, Joanna remembers, and I was unable to regain control of any aspect of my life. I started acting out in ways that I had never done before because everything seemed like it was too much of an effort. I simply didn't give a damn about anyone or myself.

Joanna was able to recover to some extent thanks to medication, therapy, a top-notch treatment facility, and her strong religious beliefs.

I battle every day to keep my symptoms under control. The my treatment facility has been extremely important to both my recovery and my life.

I have no doubt that I wouldn't be where I am today if it weren't for the staff there. I am aware that I put in the effort to get here, but they are the ones who assisted me in shifting into drive and helped me get out of a jam by pushing or even carrying me.

Today, Joanna feels that she is thriving both at home and at work.

My symptoms are under control, and I'm currently stable. A lot of work was required to get here. It took others to have faith in me.

I had to put in a lot of work to want to learn how to improve, and it took even more work to actually do it.

Nobody ever assured me that recovery would be simple, but they did give me the conviction that every bit of effort I put into it would be worthwhile.

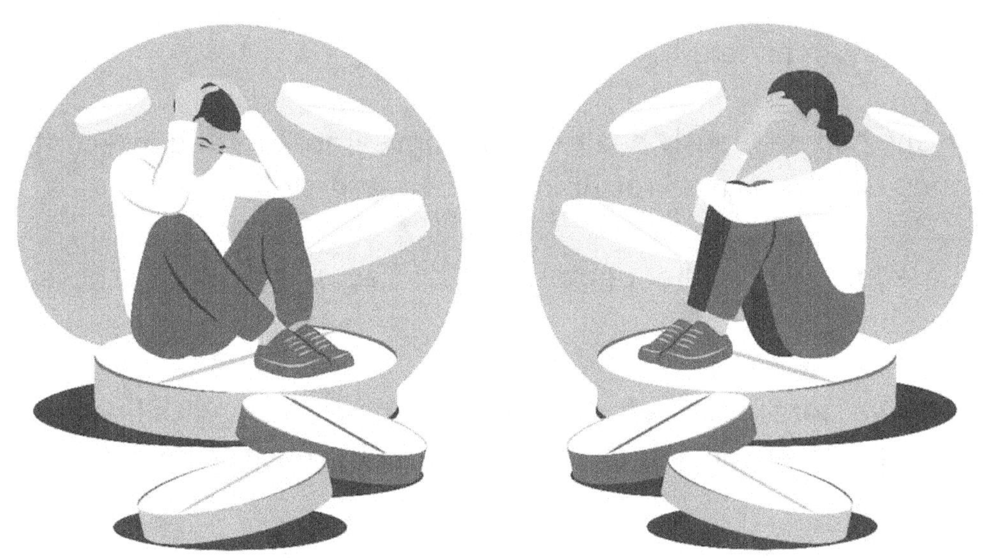

# Narrative 12 –
# Bipolar disorder, Depression Recovery: Judy's Story

## Narrative 12 - Bipolar disorder, Depression Recovery: Judy's Story

Judy believed she "had the world by the tail" after earning a bachelor's degree and a master's degree in Architecture.

Even though she had previously dealt with gloomy emotions and insecurities, she never imagined that they could result in clinical depression.

But by the time Judy was 24, her depression was having a significant negative impact on her life.

In the end, she was forced to file for bankruptcy and move in with her parents after being admitted to the hospital numerous times, losing her apartment, job, and benefits.

I genuinely believed that there was no longer any chance for me to lead a life that even remotely resembled that of a normal adult, and that I would always be a child at heart, daydreaming about the future.

Life began to improve for Judy at a hospital dialectical behavior therapy (DBT) day program, though.

Judy learned new techniques to control and cope with her emotions and tolerate emotional distress through the program's individual and group therapy (most beneficial for people who have trouble managing their emotions).

Judy's life "took a giant leap forward" when she re-entered the job market eight years after it had fallen apart.

According to Judy, since recovery is a personal endeavor, it is conceivable for the majority of people.

There is no right or wrong way to recover; instead, it is about leading a fulfilling life that is filled with ups and downs, successes and failures, dreams and hopes.

It is about creating or starting over in life after receiving a mental illness diagnosis.

*Being diagnosed as having a serious mental illness was the most disenfranchising event in my life, and I never imagined that it would also be one of the most empowering.*

# Sleep deprivation and bipolar disorder.

It makes sense that people with bipolar disorder would have trouble sleeping.

Manias are linked to days of not being tired enough to sleep, doing too much, and abusing drugs, which eventually catch up with them and keep them from sleeping.

On the other hand, the depressive symptoms of bipolar disorder are the same as those of clinical depression, which is linked to trouble sleeping on its own.

In fact, sleep problems can be a sign that an episode is coming on for many people with bipolar disorder.

A manic episode can also be caused by not getting enough sleep or even by jet lag.

Lack of sleep also makes us less emotionally strong, which makes our mood worse and makes us more likely to feel anxious or sad.

Some of the most common sleep problems caused by bipolar disorder are insomnia, less need for sleep, too much sleep, sleep apnea, delayed sleep phase syndrome, and tiredness.

Many of the effects of not getting enough sleep may sound familiar to you because they are also symptoms of bipolar disorder.

Bipolar disorder causes moodiness, bad judgment, irritability, depression, anxiety, and trouble focusing.

Since these are also caused by not getting enough sleep, the effects are worse for people with bipolar disorder.

Researchers have found that not getting enough sleep makes bipolar symptoms come back.

Losing sleep is especially bad for women with bipolar disorder because it makes them much more likely to have a manic episode.

# Insomnia or Sleep Deprivation (cont.)

**Hypersomnia:**

The opposite of insomnia is hypersomnia.

It means sleeping too much, which happens to one-third of people with bipolar disorder.

Most people with bipolar disorder have one of two types of hypersomnia:

- People who sleep 10 hours or more are said to have a "long sleep." They also spend a lot more time in bed, whether they are sleeping or not. "Long sleep" can be a sign that a bout of depression is coming.

- People who stay in bed for a normal amount of time but are still too tired during the day and wish they could get more sleep have "Excessive sleepiness". This is often a sign of mania instead of depression, but it can also be a sign of depression.

**Fatigue:**

People with bipolar disorder often feel tired all the time.

The body gets tired from the big changes in mood and energy.

Depression or trouble sleeping is often caused by fatigue.

Fatigue is especially hard to deal with because it makes you feel not only very tired but also very low on energy and not very motivated to do much of anything.

**Bipolar disorder responds well to a sleep schedule** that works with the body's circadian rhythm. Changes in the body, mind, and behavior that happen every 24 hours are called circadian rhythms.

A cheap and natural way to avoid mania and sadness is to learn how to avoid mood swings by having good "sleep hygiene."

In our hectic society, sleep adjustments are not always simple, but please know that even a few of the modifications suggested here may lessen the need for some drugs and, in the long run, avoid mood swings.

**Determine if you are serious about increasing your sleep or just like talking about it.**

You won't see big changes until you're willing to make some sacrifices in order to sleep. This isn't pleasant or fair, but concentrating on getting enough sleep at the same time every night may change your life if you have bipolar disorder.

This is particularly true for people who experience more than four mood fluctuations every year.

**Determine the cause of your sleep problems.**

Although bipolar disorder is infamous for causing sleep difficulties, not all sleep disorders are caused by bipolar disorder.

Obesity, changes in hormones, especially menopause in women, changes in testosterone due to aging in men, and physical pain can all cause big changes in sleep.

# Insomnia or Sleep Deprivation (cont.)

Recognize the relationship between sleep and bipolar disorder.

Bipolar disorder behaves similarly to a sleep problem.

Consider how your sleep changes when you are manic, or how sadness may cause you to wake up too early and then overwhelm you with thoughts, or make you so fatigued that your body feels like it is stuck to bricks.

It seems to follow that regulating sleep is the best method to treat bipolar disorder.

The body's 24-hour clock is set by the hormone melatonin, which comes out in the afternoon, and the neurotransmitter serotonin, which comes out in the morning. This is the basis for circadian rhythm sleeping.

As a general rule, try to be asleep by 11 p.m. and up by 7 a.m.

No, this will not be easy, and in many cases, you will have to say no to something you really want to do.

We often lack energy as a result of bipolar depression. Energy drinks do work at first and might help us feel better when we are depressed.

Caffeine acts as a stimulant. It interferes with sleep. Caffeine may exacerbate restlessness in those suffering from bipolar disorder.

Most people have to work, and you can't always control your schedule, but please know that research on sleep and bipolar often comes to the same conclusion: shift work, working at night, resting during the day, and/or a fluctuating schedule are not beneficial for people with bipolar.

# Insomnia or Sleep Deprivation (cont.)

It will not be easy to get your sleep in order if you have bipolar disorder, but please know that sleep management is the number one way a person with bipolar disorder can naturally, and at a very low cost, take care of many of the ups and downs associated with the condition.

**Respecting our internal clock is sound medicine.**

We suggest keeping a sleep journal for at least one week, but ideally for two to three weeks if at all possible.

# Top ANXIETY & BIPOLAR FAQ

- **What does anxiety do to someone with bipolar disorder?**
  - When a person has both, they may find that their anxiety makes their bipolar disorder symptoms worse. This could lead to: more mixed episodes of being both happy and sad. an increase in how bad mood episodes are.

- **What does bipolar anxiety feel like?**
  - Some of the physical signs of a panic attack are chest pain, heart palpitations, shortness of breath, dizziness, and stomach aches. Bipolar disorder can make panic attacks more likely. Chances that someone with bipolar disorder also has an anxiety disorder.

- **What is anxious distress with bipolar disorder?**
  - If you have bipolar disorder with anxious distress, at least two of your mood episodes are caused by anxiety. These symptoms can include being restless, not being able to focus, worrying, feeling tense, and being afraid of losing control.

- **What does stress do to a person with bipolar disorder?**
  - In a study that came out in June 2014 in the Journal of Affective Disorders, bad or stressful things in life were linked to mood swings later on. In the early stages of bipolar disorder, episodes of depression or mania seem to be more often brought on by stressful life events.

- **Can anxiety be confused with bipolar disorder?**
  - Anxiety and bipolar disorder are both mental health problems that can look and feel similar. Some people also have both bipolar disorder and anxiety at the same time. The main difference is in what causes the overall symptoms.

- **What triggers bipolar disorder?**
  - Some things can make it more likely that someone will get bipolar disorder or cause the first episode. Having a close family member with bipolar disorder, like a parent or sibling. High-stress times, like when a loved one dies or when something else terrible happens. Abuse of drugs or alcohol.

- **What is the best way to treat anxiety in a bipolar person?**
  - Cognitive-behavioral therapy (CBT), a type of psychotherapy, is thought to be one of the best ways to treat anxiety.
  - Ways to deal with stress and relax, like taking deep breaths.

- **How does the "333 rule" help with anxiety?**
  - "What are three noises you hear?"
  - Move your fingers, then your shoulders, and then your feet.
  - Say what you see three times.
  
  "If your mind feels like it's going a thousand miles per hour, try this exercise to bring yourself back to the present."

- **Can you get rid of very bad anxiety?**
  - Since anxiety is a normal part of being human, it can't be completely cured. But being anxious should be a short-term feeling that goes away when a stressor or trigger is no longer there.

- **How does a person with anxiety behave?**
  - Your anxiety is uncontrollable and distressing. Your anxiety impacts your daily life, including school, work, and social interactions. You cannot abandon your concerns. You worry about a variety of topics, including your career and health, as well as trivial matters, such as domestic tasks.

- **Is overthinking a sign of bipolar disorder?**
  - When a person with bipolar disorder enters a hypomanic or manic episode, racing thoughts are frequently one of the first symptoms to appear. It is sometimes, but not always, a debilitating experience.

- **When does bipolar disorder peak?**
  - Bipolar disorder is a persistent mental condition that often manifests between the ages of 20 and 40.

- **Can anxiety be mistaken for bipolar disorder?**
  - Patients with transient anxiety, agitation, irritability, and restlessness are occasionally incorrectly diagnosed with bipolar illness.

- **Does bipolar get worse at night?**
  - Experts still don't know everything they want to know about what causes bipolar disorder and how it affects the way people sleep and wake up. Changes in the circadian rhythm could be a cause of symptoms that seem to get worse at night, but other things could also be to blame.

- **Does anxiety go along with mania?**

  - When they have anxiety, a lot of people feel like they are a little "manic" and full of energy. But anxiety doesn't cause mania and doesn't make it worse. Mania can sometimes make people feel anxious because manic episodes themselves can be very stressful.

- **Do people who have bipolar disorder hear voices?**
  - It is not common knowledge that some people who struggle with bipolar disorder also experience psychotic symptoms. Delusions, as well as auditory and visual hallucinations, could be among these symptoms. When it comes to me, I hear voices. This takes place during times when my mood is extremely unstable, specifically when I am manic or terribly depressed.

- **What are the top five ways to alleviate anxiety?**
  - Learning about anxiety, mindfulness, relaxation techniques, correct breathing techniques, dietary adjustments, exercise, learning to be assertive, building self-esteem, cognitive therapy, exposure therapy, structured problem solving, medication, and support groups are some of the techniques that can be used to manage anxiety disorders.

- **Is schizophrenia caused by anxiety?**
  - Even though some people with schizophrenia have anxiety, people with anxiety disorders can't get schizophrenia because of their anxiety. no matter how bad their anxiety gets.

- **Can someone mistake bipolar for anxiety?**
  - Mania and anxiety can feel the same at times. Mania and anxiety can both cause problems sleeping, racing thoughts, irritability, restlessness, and trouble focusing.

**FAQ references:**

*https://www.medicalnewstoday.com/articles/bipolar-vs-anxiety*

*https://www.psycom.net/bipolar-disorder-anxiety*

*https://www.verywellmind.com/what-are-specifiers-379957*

*https://www.everydayhealth.com/bipolar-disorder-pictures/biggest-triggers-of-bipolar-mood-swings.aspx*

*https://psychcentral.com/anxiety/clinical-distinctions-between-bipolar-and-generalized-anxiety-disorder*

*https://www.mayoclinic.org/diseases-conditions/bipolar-disorder/symptoms-causes/syc-20355955*

*https://www.verywellmind.com/anxiety-medications-380539*

*https://www.healthline.com/health/bipolar-disorder/sundown-syndrome-bipolar*

*https://www.calmclinic.com/anxiety/deal-mania*

*https://www.mind.org.uk/information-support/your-stories/hearing-voices-with-bipolar-disorder/*

*https://www.betterhealth.vic.gov.au/health/conditionsandtreatments/anxiety-treatment-options*

*https://nopanic.org.uk/neurosis-or-psychosis/*

*https://psychcentral.com/anxiety/clinical-distinctions-between-bipolar-and-generalized-anxiety-disorder*

*https://www.healthline.com/health/anxiety/does-anxiety-ever-go-away*

*https://www.nhs.uk/mental-health/feelings-symptoms-behaviours/feelings-and-symptoms/anxiety-disorder-signs/*

*https://www.ncbi.nlm.nih.gov/pmc/articles/PMC2848458/*

*https://www.webmd.com/bipolar-disorder/news/20080506/bipolar-disorder-overdiagnosed*

# *Resources*

**Books**

**Manic a Narrative** - *Terri Cheney*

**Nothing was the same** – *A Narrative – Kay Redfield Jamison*

**Bipolar Disorder** – *A Family-Focused Treatment Approach – Second edition, David J. Miklowitz*

**Diagnostic And Statistical Manual Of Mental Disorders** – *Fifth Edition DSM-5*
**Living with Bipolar Disorder** - *A Guide for Individuals and Families - Michael W. Otto, Ph.D. Noreen A. Reilly-Harrington, Ph.D. - Robert O. Knauz, Ph.D. - Aude Henin, Ph.D. - Jane N. Kogan, Ph.D. - Gary S. Sachs, M.D.*

**Practical Management of Bipolar Disorder** - *Edited by Allan H. Young - Department of Psychiatry, University of British Columbia, Vancouver, Canada - I. Nicol Ferrier Institute of Neuroscience, University of Newcastle, Newcastle upon Tyne, UK - Erin E. Michalak - Department of Psychiatry, University of British Columbia, Vancouver, Canada*

**Loving someone bipolar disorder** *SECOND EDITION Understanding & Helping Your Partner JULIE A. FAST JOHN D. PRESTON, PsYD*

**Get It Done When You're Depressed**: *50 Strategies for Keeping Your Life on Track. New York: Penguin/Alpha Books. Preston, John, John O'Neil, and Mary Talaga. 2010. A Consumer's Guide to Psychiatric Drugs: Straight Talk for Patients and Their Families. New York: Pocket Books.*

**Websites**

*https://www.nhs.uk/mental-health/conditions/bipolar-disorder/overview/*
*https://www.mentalhealth.org.uk/explore-mental-health/a-z-topics/bipolar-disorder*
*https://cpa.ca/psychology-works-fact-sheet-bipolar-*
*disorder/#:~:text=In%20Canada%2C%202.2%25%20of%20individuals,both%20men%20 and%20women%20equally.*
*https://www.webmd.com/bipolar-disorder/mental-health-bipolar-disorder*
*https://my.clevelandclinic.org/health/diseases/9294-bipolar-disorder*
*https://www.nimh.nih.gov/health/topics/bipolar-disorder*
*https://www.healthline.com/health/bipolar-disorder*
*https://www.ncbi.nlm.nih.gov/pmc/articles/PMC5947163/*
*https://www.mayoclinic.org/diseases-conditions/bipolar-disorder/symptoms-causes/syc-20355955*
*https://psychiatry.org/patients-families/bipolar-disorders/what-are-bipolar-disorders*
*www.BpHope.com*
*https://www.mind.org.uk/information-support/types-of-mental-health problems/bipolar-disorder/about-bipolar-disorder/*
*www.HealthyPlace.com*